MALE PRACTICE IN A SACRED PLACE

BY

CAROLYN WILLIS

ISBN: 978-1-963502-55-8

ABOUT THE AUTHOR

Carolyn Willis is a retired individual with over 30 years of experience working with disadvantaged youth, including directing a program for teen pregnancy. She holds a degree in Criminal Justice and Psychology from Illinois State University. Carolyn finds inspiration in life experiences and a profound love for people. She actively participates in her church as a minister and choir member.

Her writing journey began with creating plays and presentations for church readings. Carolyn has a grown daughter pursuing medical studies and a son employed by the city of Chicago. She is enthusiastic about bringing creativity to life through fiction or non-fiction and aspires to write a children's book and a fictional teen character navigating faith-based families.

Carolyn's devotion to her mother, who battled dementia, reflects her compassionate nature. She managed caregiving responsibilities while continuing to write. Carolyn stresses the importance of journaling and maintaining consistent writing habits despite life's challenges.

Beyond writing, Carolyn volunteers for a senior program and enjoys socializing with friends and family, dining out, watching movies, and staying updated on current affairs.

DEDICATION

This book is dedicated to my late parents Elder Tommy and Lillian Wade. My siblings Linda Lucas, Beverly Miller, Janice Matthews, Rodney Wade and Sidney Wade. My Pastor Thomas Miller, and Betty Butler who prayed with me on this journey.

CONTENTS

"*Many will say to me in that day, Lord, Lord, have we not prophesied in thy name? and in thy name have cast out devils? And in thy name done many wonderful works? And then will I profess unto them, I never knew you: depart from me, ye that work iniquity.*" (Matthew 7: 22-23).

I did not understand Matthew 7:23; it seemed to be the scariest scripture in the Bible until I grew in God's word. It did not make sense whatsoever; how does one cast out devils, prophesied and do wonderful works in the name of Jesus and not known by God? It made me wonder what was wrong with these people. Were they just imposters, imitators, or con artists? The part that really got to me is that Jesus said he never knew them, which means these people never had a relationship with God. It surely did not mean he did not know who they were because God knows everything. God is omniscient, meaning He is All-Knowing. Proverbs 15:3 says, "*The eyes of the Lord are in every place, watching the evil and the good.*" God has given us free will and does not make us do right or wrong, and it is up to man to turn away from sin.

The title of the book came from a first sermon I delivered at Trinity Church of God in Christ, where I was a teacher. This was during a revival where Pastor Charles W. Nelson asked me to speak. I was familiar with getting before people because I was a singer and had given presentations, but I had never actually brought a sermon. I was praying and waiting on God for a word, and as I was sitting in a chair meditating, I heard "Male Practice in a Sacred Place." I had no idea what that meant in terms of church.

I knew what it meant in the professional world. I looked up what malpractice was. The dictionary describes it as an improper, illegal, negligent activity, especially by a doctor, lawyer, or public official, who causes injury. Then I looked up sacred, and it read something related to religion, treated with respect and care, and declared holy. God began to speak to me, and I wrote down all the details quickly because the spirit was clear and had conviction. My heart was excited, and I heard from Him. The Lord let me know that the church was operating below the standard of the word. This means some have left God's standards for their own way. God was saying to me that people needed healing and deliverance in every area of their lives, and the church was not always meeting the need, so people were leaving the church the same way they came in, sin-sick and hurting.

I watched a documentary casting a story about a child evangelist. It was not a show I had planned to watch, but it got my attention while I was browsing the channels. This show enlightens me more about the scripture Matthew 7:22-23. It was a story of a child evangelist and how his calling came about. It turned out his parents told him at an early age that he was called to preach and took him on the circuits where they held revivals all over the country. His parents were also evangelists and were well-known.

The young boy, whom I will call Johnny, was preaching spirited brimstone messages about sin and Hell, sounding every bit beyond his years. To tell you the truth, it was very entertaining and charismatic; I realized this child was only imitating what he saw his parents do. During the interview, he said he did not know what he was doing even though he was praying for people, and they were throwing down their walking sticks and getting out of wheelchairs. After Johnny became a teenager, he told his parents he no longer wanted to do this. He let them know you wanted me to do this, not God.

Johnny is now in his twenties and has a drug addiction without money to support it. He had friends in the same predicament, and he told them he knew how to get cash for drugs. He told them about his childhood preacher history, where he made lots of money. He said he would call some churches to inquire if he could speak, and most agreed with excitement because they remembered the young child preacher who was anointed and used by God. He ended up speaking at many churches, preaching, saying all the right things, and using the Bible. Many were large congregations where he prayed for people. They fell out in the spirit, came out of wheelchairs, and deaf ears were opened.

In watching this, you would think he was sincere because the spirit in the place appeared vigorous, the people were excited and praising God with a loud voice, and they were being healed. The interviewer asked how he was able to demonstrate such power without a call to preach. Johnny responded by saying it was not about him; it was because of the faith of the people and that God was not going to withhold His blessings.

The documentary showed the young man purchasing drugs with the money sharing with his friends. He continued this behavior with arrogance and no shame for what he was doing. I remember a Bishop stating, "God will use a can of pork-n-beans to save you," and that is how much he cares about His people. My understanding of Matthew 7:22-23 became very clear that day: "*I never knew you, depart from me, you worker of iniquity.*"

We should never take things or life for granted, what power of faith will bring about, and how someone working as an imposter can be effective in getting people to believe him to be a servant of God. It is wrong in every way to use God's name to support sin, immorality, and dishonesty, failing to represent our holy God. How is this malpractice? Remember earlier the description of how someone professional or public person who is improper, unethical, and negligent in their duties causes harm. Many leaders and members have caused harm to others by misrepresenting Christianity, and many hurt people leave the church, or some may not ever want to be involved because of the stories they have heard.

I felt sorry for the young man because his parents did not teach him how a child should go; when he was old, he would not have departed from it. Proverbs 22:6. Johnny could only go back to what he learned.

I always loved to see God's move, speaking in tongues, prophecy going forth, and healing where people who could not walk walked again or those who could not hear could hear again. I never thought people of God doing these things were not totally sold out to living a life lined up with the gospel. I am sure if I had that experience early in my walk with Christ, confidence in any church organization would be gone. I did hear of preachers beating their wives, having affairs, and getting drunk. Some of these preachers could preach and speak well, speaking in tongues. I became somewhat confused. I thought everyone speaking in tongues was holy and lived a cut above the rest of the saints.

People cannot be caught up in how someone else is living, measuring them by their own walk with God. One should never be shaken about others because the Bible talks about false prophets and those who walk after the flesh and not the spirit. One scripture that helped me with the entire matter was Romans 11:29. *"For the gifts and calling of God is without repentance."* It means that the promises and the gifts of God are irrevocable. He does not take back what He has given.

How can we do better in church? We should, of course, truly give our lives to Christ and be serious about the sanctity of God's word. How can one not reverence a Holy God Who can destroy both body and soul Matthew 10:28? We must know He is the Almighty God. Another is that we must make sure our calling and election are sure, and leaders use discernment in who to send out. The word says in 1 Timothy 5:2, *"Lay hands on no man suddenly."* Many interpret this scripture to mean that we do not lay hands on the sick or cast out devils for fear a spirit will transfer to us, but it means that leaders should not hastily ordain a person to a sacred office without giving them a chance to prove themselves suitable for Christian ministry. We should have proof that they are qualified for the position in every way and, foremost, that their lives are holy before God.

Church, keep your eyes on God and not people because you can really get discouraged when someone in high esteem fails. Continue to pray for church leaders where Satan's attack is the greatest to get the church off the mark of the high call of Jesus Christ.

I always say we have to play church or be deceptive when we can be the real church with all the blessings and promises of God. Get right church and go home.

Money, Money

"For the Love of Money is the Root of All Evil."
(1 Timothy 6:10)

I remember a friend came to visit me at my parents during my recovery from a condition of encephalitis that was to take me out, but it was not to happen. He said the Lord sent him to tell me I was his wife. The problem was that God did not tell me, and I told him so. His name was Manny Washington, and he was a loudmouth; he would holler "Wade girl" from across a room. Wade is my maiden name, and my first name is Carolyn, and this annoyed me. He would say Wade girl, you sure are fine, *my, my, my*. It was a real turnoff. I knew him as a boisterous personality, popular and smart, but not my type. We discussed what we were doing and our plans. He was a teacher, and I was a Behavioral Specialist at a group home. I aspired to go back to school for a Master's in Counseling.

What he said about his plan floored me. "You know the biggest pimp is a church pastor; he collects all that money and doesn't have to work, and that's what I want to do." I was appalled, and I responded that was wrong; a pastor is to look after God's people; it is about salvation and souls and leading people in the path of righteousness. He just laughed and asked me to marry him and to seek God's advice about me being his wife. I knew the answer, and I did not have to pray. He returned the next day and got his answer—a resounding "no!"

I have not seen Manny in years, but heard he is pastoring out of state. Hope getting money as a pimp was just an idle statement.

There is much controversy concerning money at the church; many people say that was why they did not attend church. One person said there was too much demand for money and could not afford to attend church. This has always been an excuse for those who did not want to support a pastor, but maybe not so much anymore. People say pastors always dress the best; they drive the best cars and live in big, beautiful houses. This is a problem when people think we should not take care of our poor. Luke 3:11 advises us to clothe and feed those in need. Many churches do and are blessed, but many still need to catch on to the needs of congregants in the body of

Christ. Timothy 5:12 says, *"Elders that rule well are to be considered worthy of double honor,"* especially those who work hard to preach and teach their flock. The scripture also says, "You shall not muzzle the ox while he is working, and the laborer is worthy of his wages." It requires money for our leaders to live and pay their bills. My father, Pastor Tommy Wade, pastored a Methodist church in Harrisburg, Illinois, and his payment would be in food, apples, oranges, and dairy products. My mother would not be so happy about that, being there were seven children. He would say he returned the money because those people were poor, but we were poor too.

We have all seen things we do not like about church and money, but they cannot keep us from giving. A pastor took money from the church, and a priest took spaghetti dinner monies. Both of these men served jail time; one pastor was warned by his deacons; it appeared he would take money from the offering plate while they were counting the money and put it in his pocket. He had a healthy membership with about two thousand members s he would get large amounts of money. The authorities were called, and he was arrested. The priest took spaghetti dinner money for a long time until caught, and their picture was side by side in the paper. I laughed, but it was not a matter of laughing. This causes people to avoid church.

We must also be careful when offering time; it is still a sacred part of worship. People dislike it when it is a long, drawn-out process. Taking up an offering should always be orderly. We should never know who is paying their tithes and who is not. When a line is called to pray for tithes are not right, while the rest sit as though giving an offering is not worthy of the same respect. I have seen this many times: 100 to 20 dollars lines. As a single parent, I sometimes could not get in any of the lines. I felt so bad at offering time. This means the pastor knew who was paying tithes, and it was noticeable that they were treated with more respect. I was glad when that part was over; what was sacred appeared not-so-sacred.

When I saw the salaries of famous evangelists and how much they made, I cringed. The richest in the world is worth 760 million dollars, another 150 million, and many more valued at millions. During this pandemic, I hope no one in these churches is destitute in food lines. Churches have to do the right thing for the poor. I remember visiting a young woman from our church. Her apartment was cold; she stated that her heat was off when asked about it. The amount she owed was a little over 200 dollars. If I had the money, she could have gotten it from me. It was a bad time for me, so I decided to appeal to my pastor. His answer was, "That's what welfare is for." Seeing his call for special offerings at times for the church concerned me, because a special offering was not called for her. My heart was broken.

It is disturbing when tithe payers are informed that they are protected from devour but never told that the church is to give to the poor. Deuteronomy 14:28 says, "*At the end of three years after the tithes have come forth of your increase; it shall be laid at the gate and given to the Levites, who worked in service in the temple, the strangers, the fatherless, and the widows which are within the gates, shall come and eat and be satisfied, and the Lord thy God may bless thee in every work of thine hands.*" We may not be able to help everyone, but we should at least start at the household of faith first. I will never forget how one pastor said he saw a woman come up to give an offering, and the children had holes in their shoes. He told that woman to keep the money and buy her children shoes. I thought that was honorable for that pastor; some would not have cared and welcomed the money, ignoring the children's needs.

How we remedy this is that we, as a church, should do our part by giving ten percent of our earnings increase. Research shows that most churches have only about thirty-three percent of people paying tithes, and for those who make seventy-five thousand dollars a year, only ten percent pay tithes. If one hundred percent of tithing were happening regularly, think of all we could do for the ministry and the community. We could do a lot for the poor.

In talking to my Pastor, Tommy Miller, about the success of New Life Church of Faith's tithes and offerings, he conveyed that we are always doing it God's way according to the Bible and faith. He said people should give freely and not feel ashamed because they do not have much. He felt the church should only strive on tithes and offerings to survive and never try to make people give but allow them to give freely. As Malachi 3:10 says, he stated, "*Bring the whole tithe into the storehouse, that there may be food in my house. Test me in this,*" says the Lord Almighty, "*and see if I will not throw open the floodgates of heaven and pour out so much blessing that there will not be room enough to store it.*"

Pastor Miller instituted a way for his members to give in secret by having a box at the back of the church. He felt the person with little to give was just as important as the one with whom he referred to scripture from Matthew 6:4 says, "*That your charitable deed may be in secret; and your Father who sees in secret will Himself reward you* [a]*openly.*" There are never lines for giving certain amounts; he mentioned several well-known ministries he had visited that still resort to these tactics. Once, he asked congregants to get in line to provide thousands of dollars. We discussed my experience of a nationally known evangelist who came to a Chicago church and stated that he would never be back if they did not collect a certain amount. Well, he never came back. My Pastor does not believe in filthy lucre and felt that he should display the most honest and honorable way for the church to survive without gimmicks or trickery. Many leaders use gimmicks such as "What is in your pockets, wallets, or purses? God said to give it all." A pastor testified he was careful to invite such people to his church after he was asked to write a certain amount the man mentioned that God said out of his checking account. He told the man that could not be true because he did not have a checkbook. I called a church in Atlanta for prayer during the most challenging time of my life. The prayer was anointed, and I felt the spirit of God. A few weeks later, I received a letter from the church that requested a donation starting at three hundred dollars, along with a prayer rug that was simply a piece of paper in the fashion of a carpet. They also sent a prophecy so general that it could fit anyone. I could have more prophecy if I had sent the money. To say the least, it was disappointing.

New Life Church of Faith does not use gimmicks or practice unbiblical giving. The church assembled in a beautiful renovated sanctuary housed in a mall the church owns called Heavenly Square. We can learn a lot from Pastor Tommy Miller, a man of integrity and faith who has been faithful in ministry for thirty-four years. The church has given to the community of Danville, Illinois, all those years. They feed the poor and hungry and give out food certificates every month. Also, the church donates to social causes at Laura Lee Fellowship, which has many activities for the youth. I remember my first Brownie meeting held at this community center and programs that kept teens off the street. New Life encourages the youth in education and academia by giving them five dollars for every A earned on their report cards.

Many church members talked about how they would like to do more in their communities because it gives them joy when we give back. Money should be for ministry, not to make ministers and certain other people rich. Seeing some come to Christ because of acts of kindness satisfies the soul. Leaders focusing on this make the church prosperous and aligned with God's plan. Let us get it right and go home.

Sexual Sin against Children

"Everyone of you should know how to possess his vessel in Sanctification and honor." (1 Thessalonians 4:4)

I love television during retirement, and watching more hours during this pandemic is probably not a good time to spend. People always say that watching too much television is a waste of time. Some say no enjoyment exists because it has changed significantly in the last ten years. In the '50s and '60s, there was no profanity, no sex scenes, or couples sleeping in the same bed; even Lucy and Desi slept in twin beds. Back then, television was more family-friendly. However, this family-friendliness probably will not play well in the 2020s because you really have to be selective in what you watch these days due to Satanic and occult themes that can rest in your spirit.

I go for the *Law and Order* series, which involves solving a crime. My degree is in Criminal Justice Science with a minor in psychology; my dream was to save my brothers and sisters in prison. After working with juvenile delinquents after college, I determined that was not my calling. I watch court dramas like Judge Mathias, Lauren Lake Paternity Court, and Judge Judy. I also love Forensic Files, Dateline, and Homicide Hunter. I feel vindicated when the cases are solved because many never get the opportunity to confront their abusers.

I usually put the commercials on silent because there are so many, counting eight in one break. You are not interested if you have seen it many times. One night, there was one I did not put on mute. It was announced that if the clergy have sexually abused you, call this number for a class action lawsuit. It went on to say that there were approximately ninety-six thousand cases concerning priests. This changed my mood and took me back to my friend Mattie. I was around eight years old when my cousin, who was a pastor, picked me up for church. He also picked up another young minister on the way with whom I was familiar. My cousin was an elderly man, and the young minister was in his late twenties. We went to the church, but I did not go in, as I was supposed to remain in the car. The two went into the church for about ten minutes and asked me if I wanted to visit my friend Mattie, who lived near the church, to play. I was ecstatic that she was a young girl, around eight the same age as me and attended the same elementary school. She did not belong to the church but often visited because it was close to her house.

When we arrived at her home, Pastor Eddie knocked on the door and asked if Mattie could come out and play with me; Mattie's mother looked puzzled, looking us over, but said it was ok. My pastor immediately started interrogating her and asked her to recant the story that the young minister had not touched her. She looked so frightened she was small, but she seemed to shrivel in my sight under the pressure of him questioning her. I remember her green and brown plaid jumper, thick long braids, and brown face as she looked toward the ground. Her eyes began to tear, shaking her head no until she shook her head yes and said she would take everything back. I was sad because my friend was not happy and she was crying. I did not know what it meant about him touching her. We did not play that day, and we never played again because soon after that, her family moved to another state.

The young man continued to have reports of touching young girls, even confronted by parents, but was never held accountable.

I thought about Mattie often. Did she live with anger or resentment, and did this change her life forever? Later that year, I experienced the same thing when a neighbor asked me if I wanted to see newborn kittens in his garage. He told me I could get a better look by standing in a chair. He lifted me up in the chair, and as I bent over to view the kittens, I felt a sharp pain in my crotch; he had his finger in my private part. I jumped out of the chair and ran.

I never mentioned it to my parents because we were not to go in a neighbor's yard at any time without permission. This man would bring us popcorn candy throughout the year, and my parents thought him to be a nice man, but I knew better. I never talked about it to anyone because I would be in trouble for not being obedient if I reported this to my parents. I was the bad person who caused this man to touch me that way; I am to blame. I wonder if they would believe me because he was the wonderful Caucasian man who did not leave the neighborhood when it became predominantly Black. Well, that is what my parents thought. He was friendly to our family and always spoke even though his wife did not. I felt nervous seeing him, felt ashamed, and lost trust in people. I also became quiet and unable to assert myself appropriately; I always felt anxious and guilty for a long time, even into my adult life. This was not the last time I was violated; a college classmate tried to rape me, and a pastor touched me inappropriately, so I had to leave the church. This took me aback for a while; I was devastated again. This time, I told two people in the church: one wanted me to forget and forgive, while the other stuck with me and listened. I cried in a fetal position for months and could not find the strength to finish this book. My emotions were all over the place; the past came to my thoughts again, and I felt that it had escaped me.

I understood that what the young minister had done to Mattie was wrong and meant being violated by people you least expect. I wish I could tell her both ministers have passed on after living long lives without being responsible for their actions. Such injustices are the reason I love watching shows like *Law and Order Special Victims* because offenders are found guilty of their crimes and have to pay the price. The scientific-legal term for people who have sex with children is pedophilia, described as a psychiatric disorder in which an adult or older adolescent is sexually attracted to children, abusing them where thousands are silent. I remember asking one of my clients why she did not report the sexual abuse by a family member. She replied that if I told someone, it would become real, and I wanted to feel that it had never happened. I heard stories like this over and over again in my job as a home visitor for high-risk pregnant teens, who were often abused as children, one seven years old. I know there is lots more out there, and that is shocking.

"Woe into you that harms God's children. But whosoever shall offend these little ones which believe in me, it would be better for him that a millstone was hung around his neck and that he was drowned in

the depth of the sea." (Matthew 18:6). God is not pleased with people who abuse innocent children in any way.

How many have heard that hurting people hurts others and find out some are abused as children grow up to be abusers? How many have caused God's people to stumble and error?

Many church officials can stay on their posts even when found out; many priests are moved to another parish where the offense continues. Even in the other churches, there have been times where abuse of a child, the board to decide to reject or maintain the clergy's position got a second chance to offend over again. I know of one such case. A member of a church confided in me that the teen leader of the teen ministry faked a church gathering at a hotel. He had rented a room, and when her daughter went to the gathering, he pretended others were coming. No one showed up; he raped this young girl. The woman, a single mother of the girl, met with the teen leader and the Pastor. He persuaded her to forgive him and not make a fuss because he had a wife and family. She was enraged and wanted to attack the church leader but held back. She finally agreed with the pastor. I questioned why she did not call the police because this is a crime. She answered that the pastor was a relative and that he was concerned there would be an investigation into the church. There are situations in which I think the church does not have the right to make decisions.

It has come to my mind that these people are not afraid of God. Instead, they have bypassed the Bible as if the words of truth did not exist. Scriptures such as Proverbs 1:1 say, "*The fear of God is the beginning of true knowledge, but fools despise wisdom and discipline.*" 1 Peter 1:16 says, "*Be ye holy because I am holy.*"

There are boundaries in immorality, but man wants to do what feels good to him and not make his flesh behave. According to Apostle Paul, "Nothing good lived in his flesh, though he wanted to do good, evil was always present." What are we to do as Christians? The word says to walk in the spirit, and you shall not fulfil the lust of the flesh.

We do not feed every feeling in our flesh if we are a new creature in Christ. Corinthians 5:17 says, "*Therefore if any man be in Christ he is a new creature, Old things are passed away, behold all things become new.*"

Some sexual predators go to places such as schools and churches for that purpose. They are opportunist who look for situations that put them close to those they are attracted to, as a priest who prey on children.

I met a woman who went to church just to get close to pastors. She told me one was her husband and that God said he was. I rebuked her by saying, "No, he isn't; he is someone else's husband, and God does not go against Himself or His word. After that conversation, she never talked to me again. God would never go against His word. Matthew 5:27 -28 says, "*You shall not commit adultery, and that everyone that looks on a woman or a (man) with lustful intent has already committed adultery in his heart.*" The seventh verse in the commandments, "You shall not commit adultery." God is not taking back His word for us.

I can go on with countless stories of betrayal, men and women leaving for another, pregnant girls in the church by the clergy.

How do we remedy this? It is just as simple as this: live as God's word says. Love your neighbor as you love yourself. Do you think the man who violated my friend Mattie wanted his children to be victims? He did not allow his children to stay all night with people. He protected them in every way. How do I know is because of that young minister I knew personally.

You have to educate your children about people who are not in their best interest and ensure they have your trust because many children don't think their parents will believe them.

Guess what? A notification on Facebook read," Abused by the clergy call this number. Notification said there were 96 thousand cases involving priests. This accounts for those who reported; believe me, there are thousands more out there. It is said that one abuser usually abuses 100 children before being caught. This Ad was everywhere now.

I was embarrassed for the notice to be on social media because millions of people will see this loss of hope in organized religion. I was also happy because this cannot be tolerated in the dark. The place where we find refuge and healing is in the headlines and is being scrutinized. People are looking at us, and that is dismal. When visitors come to the church with young children, we suggest taking them to the children's church or the nursery; they sometimes reply that they do not allow their children to go until they can verbalize.

It is understood and not challenged as much because you cannot explain that the man in the suit, the robe, the smiling pristine dressed nursery worker, the deacon, and the choir member are ones you can trust based on looks. Lately, there have been women who have violated children and do not meet the description of a predator. It is not just men that we are concerned about. Women are guilty, and some judgment has been lenient. A teacher had sex with young students, the argument made, she was too pretty to go to prison. They would never say a man is too handsome to be in prison. We cannot have a double standard for this.

Presently, there is a priest in Chicago accused of molesting brothers. He is much loved for working for social justice in the black community and coming to the city's aid for the disenfranchised, the poor, and the inner-city youth. You sometimes wonder why it took so long to report the incident. Because children are frightened, it is just as simple as that.

Fright is why children do not report adults violating because who will believe them? The story becomes real, or someone may get hurt. I know that because of the incident with our neighbor, I kept to myself for years because my father would have put some hurt on the neighbor. Maybe the drama of it all would have been too overwhelming, and truthfully, an adult is powerful to stand against if no one believes your story.

No one should ever say they did not have the ability to abuse a child because of title or reputation unless present. We are not talking about the Boogeyman or a monster but, many times, a well-standing person in the community. Some teachers, social workers, politicians, police, preachers, pastors, and deacons have been guilty.

In watching a PBS special, a Black woman named Sarah from Kentucky is fighting against child marriages; I discovered you could marry a child with parental consent in 48 States. The story goes that a Bishop raped Sarah when she was merely eight years old and became pregnant at the age of 10 when a deacon, who was in his 20s, was forced to marry at the age of 11 with the consent of her mother and by the signature of a judge.

The young woman ended up being in an abusive relationship and had five children with her husband. It was hard to get away from him because she was too young to work, and the babies kept on coming. She said she felt entrapped and hopeless. She was not able to secure a lawyer because a child cannot file for the desolation of marriage until 18 years of age. She finally got out of the relationship and expressed not being able to converse with her mother or anyone because people in her community deemed it better for her to be married than to be a single mother. They did not consider her raped but looked upon her as a characterless girl. Believe me, when you see a girl at the age of 11 pregnant, there is something very wrong not just with people but with the entire society. That child had her innocence thwarted by an older man.

She is a beautiful woman today who is striving to advocate for young women in forced marriages. Sarah has been to the Capital and talked to Senators and Representatives who did not think children getting married upon pregnancy was a problem. The part they were not aware of was that some of those children were 11 and 12 years old. She stated that many states were not aware that this was even happening.

Kentucky is one of the states where, under certain conditions, a child can get married, and no bride or groom is too young. In many states, 17 and younger have consent from parents and judges. Nine states, including Kentucky, waive the minimum age requirement for girls who are pregnant. Generally, we blame Middle Eastern or

African countries with the highest rates in Chad, Guinea, Bangladesh, etc. The Central African Republic and Nepal are above 50%. Saudi Arabia, South Sudan, and Yemen do not have a minimum age for marriage.

We assume that child marriage is a thing of the past, says the senior council of a Virginia advocacy group, pushing for the age to get married at 18. Just recently, Missouri State Senator Mike Moon defended marriages at 12 years of age. He stated that a couple that married when they were twelve still married. He felt this was ok if a female became pregnant. This included grown men who committed statutory rape. Texas has the highest rate of child marriages in the nation. About 40 thousand children were married between the years of 2012-2014. The officials said some of the men are much older and cited an incident where the child was 15 and he was 53. He groomed her on the internet. The council stated it seemed pedophilia, rape, and human trafficking were under the approval of a judge. These children were not able to finish their education and were subjected to poverty, mental health issues, and higher incidents of domestic violence.

My paternal grandfather stated that his first wife was thirteen when he married her. He said that his food was not ready when coming home after work; he would take off his belt and whip her. He told it matter-of-factly, as normal as washing his face. I could not help but feel a sense of repulsion, but that was in his day. It was legitimate to marry a child in the 1900s; even in the '60s, families would sweep stuff like this under the rug. If she became pregnant, marriages were forced—they called them shotgun weddings, where it implied the girl's father had a shotgun at your wedding until the "I do" was said.

When working with single teenage girls, I tended to hug them out of empathy and because of seeing their pain and struggle. One particular time, I went in to hug a client, but she resisted and stepped back. She explained that she did not like hugging. That felt awkward; I did it without understanding until I went to a training session on how to build relationships with the population we served. We learned to ask permission for hugs and interaction with the babies. The young client who resisted my hug disclosed to me that she was molested as a child. After six months of building a relationship, my client allowed me to hug her and the baby.

We are dealing with our children experiencing post-traumatic stress disorder or PTSD. This should not be for innocent children trying to find themselves in the world and being lost in adults' problems. Yes, sick adults hurt our children. When asked, predators reported molested as children suffering from low self-esteem.

How do we protect our children? Education about what a violation of our space and body is helpful. Have a code for strangers; no one should be able to persuade your child to leave with them unless they possess the code you have given. Teach your children never to help a stranger look for a pet or take candy and gifts. Please encourage them to be in groups because most predators want a lone victim. Teach them not to be afraid to report anyone inappropriate to them.

Those who can take the lead are parents, teachers, social workers, and churches concerned about the welfare of children. Parents should always be suspicious of people who are more involved with children instead of adults; a grown person who wants to be with children and not adults is not normal. Ask God for the gift of discernment, watch and pray, and do not allow your child to be with anyone you do not know. When she was about ten years old, my daughter had a friend at school she talked about all the time. She said this friend wanted her to stay all night; my answer was "no." She was adamant about me letting her go, but my answer remained the same. One day, the mother and daughter ended up at my door, begging me to let her go. I explained that I did not know them well enough for my daughter to stay all night. They looked nice enough, but as I said before, looking nice does not matter to me. We lived in Normal, Illinois, which is pretty much a white neighborhood, and they were white too. I did not want them to think I was biased, but I needed to protect my daughter. We watched the two girls at the door in tears, our hearts broken, and we could see it in the mother's eyes. When they left, my daughter was crying, "Why, why?" and the only thing I could come up with sounded crazy; "I don't know them, and they may sacrifice you to the gods." She understands very well what I mean now; back then, it was ridiculous.

Every day in the news, we see children kidnapped, trafficked, raped, and murdered. There was one report where a man tried to grab a child out of a mother's arm. She fought for her baby and won. He ran off, and it was caught on cameras. Thank God for cameras. Weak people should avoid tempting situations like not going to a park to watch children and going on the internet searching for illicit information. Praying gives you strength and stability in your daily lives. One should hold oneself to the highest moral standards and practice self-discipline. One should redirect one's passion by visiting places surrounded by strong people, praying, and reading the word of God. The church has the responsibility to report all abuse to the police. This is something you do not want to handle on your own because children's lives can be ruined forever. Church watch and pray, and have training and background checks for childcare. That is a reality because the world is much more unpredictable and violent now. Let us get right and go home.

POWER AND LOVE

*"Having a form of Godliness but denying the power thereof;
from such turn away." (2 Timothy 3:5)*

Have you ever felt the church of yesterday is a memory rather than an existence? I have talked to people who felt that being in Christ seemed more serious and invested in the former days. We were hungry for the things of God. It was our life, and when I say it was our life. We breathed and lived our lives as believers. We shared our testimonies, our food, and our time. No one was embarrassed if their homes were not furnished with the finest things or if the cars driven were noisy and clunky. The richness of God's presence was more important. When we went to church, God would meet us there because we anticipated He would show up, and He did. It was nothing for many to come to Christ, healed or filled with the Holy Spirit. The church was exciting, and I did not miss the life that I had lived before this.

I was enjoying the journey and loving God and his people. Getting ready for church felt like Christmas morning to me; my son and daughter felt the same. This was because I went to church again after about ten years of indulging in worldliness. Before, I sent the children on a church bus that picked up families on campus. While they were gone, I would have friends over playing cards, listening to Frankie Beverly, Earth Wind and Fire, Marvin Gaye, and all the hit songs of that time. When they returned, they would tell me what the pastor had preached. My daughter, being the spokesperson, reported that the pastor said if your parents are drinking and sleeping around, they are going to Hell.

As she was talking, she was pouring out my drink. My son, not so vocal, shook his head in agreement. He was a quiet soul who did not like to talk much, and for some reason, I wanted to hear him say something to the matter. My daughter is the complete opposite; she is bold and will speak what is on her mind even though she is sweet-natured. They relayed the message while we were playing cards. I laughed, but my friends said it was not funny, and left my apartment quickly; begging them to stay one replied that we are gone if a child can tell you this. Soon, I started going back to church, and I have my children to thank for that.

Both of my children gave their lives to Christ. My son was eleven, and my daughter was eight years old. It was the same day I reclaimed my faith as well. We would read the Bible, pray, enjoying church at home. It was nothing for them to hear me sing and praise God loudly on any given day. The church was the same way and had no fear of affirming their faith. My new friends would openly talk and expound on the scriptures. These people really believed in living a life pleasing to God. People would say it does not take all that, but I said this: it took more for me because of my battles and fights for the things I needed to overcome. I had a weakness: I liked men, and they wanted me. Do I need to say more?

We were also very active in the community, a college town where most of us attended Illinois State University, including myself. Witnessing was an avenue we used to get another student to join us at our church, Roberts Memorial, which was held on campus. The joy of soul winning put us on a high, and we rejoiced when one gave their life to Christ. We had a group of dedicated people who would go out on campus spreading the good news of the gospel.

Holiness was also a word I had not heard in a long time as if it were old-fashioned in some churches. One reason is that in some churches, outward appearances seem more important than men's hearts. Some think this means attending a church wearing your dresses to the ground, no make-up, no movies, and for some people, it means no television and, of course, no dating. This church taught holiness and its meaning.

In researching holiness and receiving the true meaning of being set aside, sacred and pure, that inputs righteousness and clean living, one that had left the life of sin to live with the character of Christ. 1 Peter 1:16 says, "Be ye holy for I am holy." That's Jesus speaking to his followers to be like him. Jesus, without sin and love, I wanted more of that teaching.

There was talk of sanctification. Some saints' understanding of what that means was amiss. Mentioning that we were sanctified insulted a mother at church who had equated the term to mean rules for women, such as wearing clothes that cover you up all over, no arms showing, long skirts or dresses, and shouting and speaking in tongues. She said, "We do not do that here," but we agreed that our dress should be modest. All churches should have the characteristic of sanctification because John 17:17 says, "We are sanctified by the word," transforming our lives from the inside out and allowing God to prepare us for His use. We also should be under pastors and teachers who can help us understand the word. Without teaching, God's power is not learned. Reading, studying the word, and praying to God for understanding are key to learning about God's character and His will for our lives. This helps us grow strong in faith and power.

It is challenging for new members to process where they belong or what church rules are. I did not have appropriate clothes because they did not wear pants to Sunday service, even if you could wear them elsewhere. The Women of Zion learned of my needs in our meeting; this group brought me gently used clothing and some new ones. I now had nice things to wear and felt the love that kept me wanting to continue to go. I also learned more about holiness and sanctification and was transformed by John 17:17. I sat under good teaching and mentoring. These women were remarkable. I realized that you must have a pastor and teaching to get strong. This is the first step in getting power in your life. I also learned to spend time with God in prayer and to study myself approved unto God. I felt welcomed there and thought they cared about my spiritual growth. The one thing that impressed me the most while at this church was that God is love, and we are to translate that love to others. Compassion moved Jesus to react to people's needs. Jesus, because of his love, many people followed him. You can feel love if the church has that gift to draw people.

First Lady Beverly Miller of New Life Church of Faith told me about her experience with a church's lack of love. She stated that she was targeted with judgments on everything, including her dress and hairstyle. She mentioned they even criticized how she directed the choir. They would say the person who had the position before her had more anointing. Lady Beverly was so happy when her husband said they were leaving, she shouted. They actually went to start New Life Church of Faith about thirty-five years ago, and many people did not support their move.

Linda Lucas recalled an incident where she was met at the door at a visiting church by a woman who told her, "You can't come in here with that eyeliner on your eyes." The woman exclaims that she is not a Christian and questions her church affiliation. When giving her church information, others joined the conversation, saying that church is not right and that they need to get it right. Remember that these people think holiness and sanctification involve the outer appearance and sometimes exclude the person's transformed life and heart for God.

If we could understand that division keeps us from having the power of God operating in our lives, we would view unity more seriously. It would bring many coming to Christ, healed, delivered, and made free. I once invited a woman to church. She asked how we take the sacrament and if we washed our feet; I told her we drink grape juice and never washed feet. She said she could not come to our church because they did not take anything off the grape and washed her feet. Many things divide us in the Christian church: the day we should worship, some say Saturday, and others Sunday. Many believe a woman's hair is covered in worship service. The greatest divider is baptism, the controversy of being baptized in Jesus's Name or the Father, son, and the Holy Ghost. When I moved to a different city, a woman told me to get it right.

I remember when visiting a church, I found a seat with other church members from my church. A woman stood over me with a threatening stare. I looked up at her, wondering what the problem was. She threw her head in the air and stomped off. I asked what was wrong, and someone said I was in her seat. I discovered some places you should not sit because that seat is a place someone has claimed. If she had mentioned it as her seat, there would not have been a problem for me to move. I hope she was able to receive the service because she looked quite salty.

These are some of the behaviors I was not used to: the judgments, the alienation of those in the same faith, and overall rudeness toward God's people. If we are not demonstrating Godliness with love, we kill fruit that generates power.

It all boils down to something God hates: pride and arrogance. The Pharisees asked Jesus about the disciples not washing their hands before eating, which was a tradition of purification. This allowed Jesus to teach about hypocrisy. They were implying that they were not keeping the law of their fathers. Jesus reminded us that the Pharisees did not keep the commandments of God of honoring their mothers and fathers. Jesus taught the lesson that traditions did not make a man clean. The Pharisees felt that eating food with unclean hands defiled them, but Jesus said it is not what goes in a man that defiles him but what comes out of him. Matthew 15:11 says, "It is not what goes into the mouth that defiles a man but what comes out of mouth defiles a man." In Matthew 15:18, Jesus says, "Those things which comes out of the mouth comes from the heart, evil thoughts, murder, adulteries, fornication, thefts, false witness, blasphemies: These are the things which defiles a man: but to eat with unwashed hands defile not a man."

The Pharisees had a form of godliness, holding on to the outward religion but denying the power in front of them as the Savior of the world. The amplified Bible says, "Holding to a form of (outward) godliness (religion) although they have denied its power (for their conduct nullifies their claim of faith). Avoid such people and keep far from them (2 Timothy 3:5).

We allow tradition to make us religious to the point that we have forgotten what true worship is all about.

What is true worship? It can only exist if it is truthful in every aspect with God. We are able to worship God in spirit and truth because the truth of Jesus is revealed to us.

Religion attracts many rules and regulations, and to please God, they exhibit outward performances and think they will touch his heart. Our outward works are an easy way out, and we can be deceived that we are pleasing God. We really forget who Jesus is; he is a spirit who wants to commune with us and have an honest relationship. Our true worship brings God into our presence. It cannot come with a form of godliness.

A form of godliness is just an open display of behaviors and attitudes contrary to God. Christians deny the power of God by honoring him with their mouth but dishonoring him through their lives. They present themselves as Christians but live in sin. Paul said he was not ashamed of the gospel because it is the power of God unto salvation, Romans 1:6. Because of the power of God's word, it should be exalted and obeyed. Living according to God's word gives us strength and resilience. A pastor once implied he would not lay hands to pray because he was unclean due to his indiscretion. Who would sacrifice not experiencing the power of God in their lives for a title?

We moved to the Chicago area and missed my old church. It was not perfect, but I always felt love and the Spirit of God.

I was really disappointed at a church with 500 members, and only eight people showed up for prayer, where power lives and breathes. If there is no prayer, there is no power.

This is what I saw: a very colored coordinated choir, a beautiful sanctuary, beautifully dressed people, auxiliaries (Mother of the church, ushers, pastors, aide ministers, elders, choir) sitting in their places waiting to execute a program that occurs every Sunday in the same order—prayer, scripture, announcements, choir selections, offering, preaching, benediction. Nothing different. A program followed to a point where they would miss it if God moved.

Love for God's ways, not our own, moves us out of tradition because God is love. We should devote more time to being the church than going to church. I am not saying to forsake the assembly but to take the church to others. That is what Jesus did: being kind, showing love, and helping dying souls.

Jesus said, "Go out into the highways and the hedges and compel men to come in so that my house may be filled." The Love of God should make us want others to have what we have, just not our friends, family, the properly dressed, those that smell good but to those under the bridge, the homeless, the wayward people with maladaptive behaviors, the alcoholic, the drug addict, the one who just seemed not to fit in. I remember we went into a bad neighborhood to pick up children for vacation Bible school. The vacation Bible school organizer advised us not to pick them up anymore because of the neighborhood and behaviors. Some of them appeared rambunctious, hungry, asking for food, and not accustomed to going to church. A few of us talked about it, but the advice came from the Pastor. We did not fight for these children, so I was disappointed in myself. Where was the compassion?

Jesus was moved by compassion and went into action. Jesus, seeing the crowd of 5,000 following him, was tired and hungry near the Sea of Galilee. He asked the disciples to get them food. The disciples asked to send them away so they could buy their own food, but Jesus said he would feed them. (Matthew 14:13 -21). When you have feelings for one's struggles and can identify them, you show love for that brother or sister; even though compassion is not love, it is a component of love. That day, two fishes and five loaves of bread Jesus miraculously fed thousands.

Two blind men followed Jesus, crying, "Have mercy on us, Son of David." He touched their eyes, and sight returned, showing compassion. (Matthew 9:27).

Jesus did not have a problem with the woman with the issue of blood. He did not react to the tradition of the prescribed routine of her cleansing. The woman's bleeding was unclean, and according to custom, she could not touch a man or a man touch her. (Luke 8:42-48).

If we were to put on the character of Jesus and show the love needed, we would have power and no longer be with just a form of godliness. I would do all that is necessary to be like Christ for the edification of the Saints. Philippians 2:5 states, "Let this mind be in you which was also in Christ Jesus."

What does it mean to have the mind of Christ? It means having the Holy Spirit, identifying with Christ's purpose, and bringing glory to God by witnessing love and grace. It also means you have the fruit of the Spirit working and cultivated in your life. Galatians 5:22 reads, "Is love, joy, peace, longsuffering, gentleness, goodness, faith, meekness, temperance: against there is no law."

Verse 23 goes on to read, "And they that are Christ's have crucified the flesh with the affections and lust. If we live in the Spirit, let us also walk in the Spirit."

If we have these characteristics, we put them on the mind of Christ. I know what to work on in my life; something has crept up. In this climate of separation and divide in politics and racism. I begin to despise people instead of the enemy, Satan, who has sown this discord. I did not want to pray for those who despitefully used the system of this world to continue oppression. Jesus prayed for those who crucified him on the cross, so who are we not to do the same? Jesus said forgive them for they know not what they are doing, Luke 23:34. Jesus was putting into practice what he preached. He was concerned for the forgiveness of those who were among the enemies. This is how we put on the mind of Christ. The church can no longer be a head count or money count but those concerned about the souls of people who are truly hurting in this day and time we are living in. During the pandemic of 2020, COVID-19 has killed almost half a million people in America, cost millions of jobs and homes, and created food insecurities we have never seen before. Many churches have come to the rescue of many, and that is the mind of Christ. This is how we become Godly with power.

I have found that the Church of Worship is not perfect, but it has all the elements that I have been looking for: the teaching of holiness and sanctification, fellowship of loving believers, outreach in the community, praying for others, feeding the poor and people giving because they love God and not because of gimmicks. Pastor Thomas Miller had COVID-19; he was on a ventilator and was on the brink of death. Corporately, the church fasted and prayed, and our pastor came through with a mighty testimony of how God brought him back. The church became concerned about others, not their own afflictions during this time. Sometimes, it takes sacrifice to see the power of God. It is no more me but Paul and Christ within me.

Love of God and others brings about the Power of Christ in our lives, not traditions, gimmicks, or selfishness.

Let us go back to being sincere about the things of God, and the church will have power. Let's get right and go home.

RACISM IN THE CHURCH

"There is neither Jew nor Greek, there is neither bond nor free, there is neither male nor female, for you are all one in Christ Jesus." (Galatians 3:28).

The most segregated hour is Sunday morning service. This is true and understandable. People tend to be more comfortable with people they look like and share the same values. The problem is when race prevents one from worshiping with people who do not look the same. We need to practice on earth because there is no such thing as a Black or White heaven or Hispanic, Indian, or Asian heaven. There is only one heaven wherein Revelations reads, "I beheld a great multitude, which no man could number, all nations and kindred, and people and tongues, stood before the throne before the Lord clothed with white robes and psalms in their hands. They cried out loudly, saying Salvation to our God, which sits upon the throne, and unto the Lamb.

There were some organized religions, once stating blacks did not go to heaven but have since changed their doctrine. Thank God for the sake of salvation for those people. The Bible says, "To love your neighbor as yourself" (Mark 12:32). People still get confused about who their neighbors are.

I did not detect any discord or friction among the multicultural church we attended. It seemed what I expected in heaven. More Blacks and Hispanics were becoming part of the ministry. The choir racially mixed and became noticeably more black. The music sounded more gospel, and more people expressed that they did not like the change. On one Sunday, the pastor announced that some complaints were made and that some did not like the changes, especially the music, and did not want to worship with us. They wanted to start their own church. He said it was fine because God had given him people of color to pastor. My heart sank, and I could not believe what I was hearing: racism in the church. How can this be?"

It is a shame that people can think they are heaven-bound with this attitude. Where is the preaching against racism? Where is the gospel of peace among the brothers? God is not happy with this. I do not watch some ministries for this reason. The church has not addressed this issue yet, but a few have. I pray that my thoughts are not plagued by hating my brothers and sisters each night. Yes, church, we are brothers and sisters, whether Black, White, Brown or Yellow. As a Black woman, I have no right to hate because, historically, people are judged because of the color of their skin. We may have some real deep feelings and hurt due to mistreatment for centuries, but we still have to pray that the system of racism is eradicated and love takes precedence.

God does not regard race or gender. He is more concerned about the spirit of man and our hearts; Galatians 23:28 reads, ' *'There is neither Jew nor Greek, neither bond nor free, neither male nor female, but all are one in Christ Jesus."*

I tried not to like my white brothers and sisters but felt that if they did not love me, why should I love them? I even did not like some of my own brothers and sisters of color if they lived a life that disgusted me. This went on for a few weeks, debating in my head. I talked to the television because it was not the real world, and I could express myself any way I wanted. I remember a co-worker said her father was so prejudiced that when seeing a Black on TV, he turned the station. This was in the '70s, and there were not as many on as there are today, so if he were living, he might have just given up watching television by now. I thought it was good for me to try to see how it felt.

Turning channels every few seconds drove me crazy, so I ended up watching animal documentaries. Turning back to regular stations and fussing at everyone made me seem rather mental. The conclusion that being racist can become a mental health issue bothered me. I was taking a week to find people disgusting, ugly, immoral, and ungodly with an abnormality of color. I reasoned with myself that color is a curse; going to the story in the Bible, when Marion and Aaron made fun of Moses' wife, who was of color, God struck them with leprosy. I had to justify my reasoning as others judged other groups. I was wrong; I was just wrong to do this.

The test I put myself through made me sick. My spirit was off. I did not feel right, and I became agitated, mentally disturbed, and out of step with God.

This was wrong, and I knew it. I dare feel this way, crying out to God and asking for forgiveness. The Holy Spirit would not allow me to foster evil thoughts. My peace returned to me, and I knew God had heard me and had forgiven me.

I now visit a multicultural church mainly because I believe in that. Heaven is a place of many kindred as the Apostle John had seen a multitude which no man could number, of all nations, and kindred, and people and tongues, stood before the throne, and before the Lamb, with angels, elders and four beasts before the throne worshipping God.

Bigots have to be miserable in this world because there are so many people and cultures; seeing this has to make them feel uneasy. We as people may think we have a right to feel hate because of mistreatment. We still have to pray for those who despitefully use us and let God fight our battles. I am not talking about not fighting for our rights through appealing to social injustice. The word says faith without works is dead alone.

The conclusion is that man lives in fear of each other, afraid they will lose rights or privileges or give up something to share God's blessing for us. If we did it in God's way, man would have everything he needs. Our country can experience blessings beyond measure. God has promised his people that if they seek him and his righteousness, all things will be added unto them (Matthew 6:33). Instead of doing it God's way, we are so busy seeking our own way that we miss the mark. We missed the mark of not loving our neighbors as we love ourselves. The practice is down here on earth because God is not going to have a Heaven for certain groups of people, nor heaven defiled by hate. God is love and made man in his image; we better put it on our clothing of righteousness. Matthew 22:37-40 reads, "*Thy shall love the Lord thy God with all thy soul, and with all thy mind."* This is the first and greatest commandment. The second like unto it, thou shall love thy neighbor as thyself. On these two commandments hang all the law and the prophets." This says that if you love God, you will love others. Let us get to the right church and go home.

DIVORCE

"I hate divorce, says the Lord God of Israel." (Malachi 2:16)

God never intended married couples to get divorced, but this occurs due to the hardening of the heart. Statistics say that 50% of all marriages end in divorce. The Barna survey average for faith-based divorce cites born-again Christians at 34%, Jewish at 30%, and Muslim at 31%. The 2021 report shows that faith-based people still have a lower divorce rate than unbelievers, and people of faith appeared the happiest. This was news before new statistics in 2023 that say 50% of Christian marriages end in divorce. How happy can that be?

Malachi 2:16 states, "*God hates divorce not only because he ordained it but because it represents our relationship with Him.*" God describes marriage in Genesis 2:24, "*When one man, Adam, and one woman, Eve, united and became one flesh.*" Biblically, there are two concepts of marriage. The couple is married in the eyes of God; Adam and Eve is this example. The marriage is in the eyes of God after they have participated in a formal ceremony. "If any man is behaving improperly to his virgin and has passed the flower of her youth, they should get married." In other words, if you are intimate before marriage, the man is to marry his virgin; they have not sinned. (1 Corinthians 7:36). People will argue that God intends for us to enjoy sex without marriage when the Bible makes it clear we are to be intimate with our mates only. Hebrews 13:4 notes that the marriage bed is honorable kept pure, and reserved for husbands and wives; all others are defiled as immoral where God will judge.

When we dissolve our marriages, it is a break with God's covenant. Marriage is regarded as a sacred institution for life. Taking the marriage vows, we say until death do us part. The sad part is that Christian marriages are ending at an alarming rate long before death. Our relationship with God should be for life, just as we do with marriage.

Jesus recited that Moses allowed divorce due to the hardness of man's heart, but not in the beginning. (Matthew 19:8). When your heart hardens, you have lost your tender heart. You are no longer kind to one another and forgiving. Ephesians 4:31 says, "*Let not bitterness, and anger, and wrath, and clamor and evil speaking be put away from you with all malice and be kind one to another tender hearted forgiving one another even as God for Christ sake hath forgiven you.*" We think this is for everyone but the one we are closest to. Many treat people outside of the family better.

God wants tender-heartedness in all relationships, especially marriage. We take our marriages for granted and will treat outside people with the utmost respect and lack the same for our husbands and wives.

The main reasons for divorce are these issues: communication, finances, lack of emotional support, emotional abuse, infidelity, and arguments.

I will address communication first; you have to be able to talk with each other and have truthful communication. I can only speak about my experience. My marriage started with a problem I should have thought about before committing. My future husband had not even told me his first name; he said, "By the way, my first name is James, not Charles. I never liked the name, so I never used it." I felt uneasy when he told me, but I did not think it was enough to call things off. What a mistake this was because, for 24 years, he had secrets and did things that he did not communicate truthfully. He would always say you know I am secretive, but you cannot hold things vital to yourself. He never was accurate about his income and once quit working and never told me he quit. He did, however, find another job. He owed a large amount of child support, which he never disclosed; I found out because a letter came stating twenty-six thousand dollars owed. Upon questioning, he did not want to talk about it. It was just lies and deception because she won the case against him. Yes, we argued a lot due to a lack of communication. It was more than I could bear. I forgave him for every act of betrayal, hoping things would improve, but not so. Our arguments were more power struggles rather than solution-oriented. We would accuse the other for every fault. I wanted to be upfront about our business, but he wanted not to discuss anything.

We never agreed on the discipline of the children; what he thought should be disciplined, I did not agree with. It was hard because my discipline pattern was already in effect; I was stern but not harsh, fair but not patronizing. He felt I was too easy. Being in the military, he had a more rigid style that my children were not used to, and there were constant conflicts.

Betty Smith stated that her communication with her husband was problematic because of his mother. It seemed her mother-in-law would say things to her that the husband should communicate. When Betty would talk to her husband, he responded that his mother meant no harm. The marriage was broken because of this, and they divorced. Third-party communication is never good and should never influence your marriage.

When I did my in-home education about communication styles with teenagers, I would present a lesson that addressed communication methods. It would ask if you yell when trying to solve a problem. Do you sulk and not do anything, calmly talk things out, or take care of a situation immediately? Some would say they would not discuss it with family or boyfriend, some said they would yell and curse, and some said they met the situation head-on. Most stated they learn their communication at home. Now, I was going to teach them how to be more effective in talking to family, friends, and boyfriends. The technique was Reality Therapy, a communication that uses open-ended questions to get one to make his own decisions and be responsible. Instead of arguing, you say I feel hurt, not you hurt me rather than saying, you need to do this, but what do you want to do? I remember a client asked me if she should get an abortion; I wondered what she wanted to do, putting it back on her to make the decision. Someone may say you have too much makeup on. Your response would be to tell me your idea of too much. This gives a person an opportunity to talk. They can say to use a little less blue on your eyelids and less red lip. Your answer could be thank you, maybe I will try that, or it could be I am just fine. I reassure you that there will not be an argument, and it will leave the person evaluating himself. A client mentioned she held things in and hoped that things would work out eventually.

When I asked how that was working, using Reality Therapy, she stated it was not. She stated feeling frustrated with the build-up of anger. We worked out a plan for her to deal with this. Another client stated that she and her partner yelled and argued, but she stated that was how her family dealt with issues. One day, I heard it over the phone when I was angry at Mom for refusing to babysit. She actually tried to get me to talk with Mom. This was not my role as a home visitor; she would take it out on her boyfriend, yelling and cursing. I asked if it was working, and she stated, "That's all I know." Some girls stated they would pout, go to their rooms, and not talk. There were a few who said they talked things out. Sometimes, these are behaviors in marriage.

We actually learn how to communicate at home, and when marrying, the pattern is carried into the marriage. I went over reality therapy principles with the girls and hope they use them to improve communication. The lessons learned hopefully will help them in the future.

We never really want to count to ten when we need to because the spirit is willing, but the flesh is weak. We should never say things to hurt or discourage but use language that builds each other up. Words such as, you are great, my hero, and doing a good job, I appreciate you. Notice that the word you was only to give accolades.

When there is no open and honest communication, the marriage will die. A real warning sign that the marriage hurts is when you stop talking altogether.

Another problem is financial compatibility, which some couples do not have. Couples may never talk or take for granted that everything will be fine. My only conversation with my ex was when he said, "I know who is going to take care of the money." I replied, "Whom?" He never answered, so I felt it should be me. Besides, my mother took care of the money and did a really good job of it. I took after my mom, and being a single parent, I took care of business. I actually worked myself through college and nurtured two children, and we never missed a meal, and they had pretty much what they needed. It turned out I was wrong. His feeling he would be better at it. We decided he would handle the family finances, but it did not work out. He was not good at paying bills on time. One day, while watching television, the lights went out, so I called the power company because I thought we had an outage. It was not so; the bill had not been paid and did not get better, so we decided to split responsibilities. He said he never paid the bills until a red slip. If you are not familiar with this, when you are delinquent, your bill will include a red slip, generally saying that your services will be discontinued if you do not pay this bill by a specific date. This was our first argument because it actually happened while watching television when the power went out. I thought it was a power outage, so I called the electric company and discovered the bill had not been paid. I had issues, too, because I liked to see where my hard-earned money was spent.

I felt more responsible, paid bills on time, and maintained two teenagers plus a husband. I mentioned a budget he wanted no part of; every family needs a budget to see where money is going and what they can do better to spend. I never knew where the money went, so I opened my own account. Our biggest fault was that we never discussed money or finances before marriage—another mistake for couples not knowing the credit score of their future spouse. I found out my husband's not paying bills was something of a habit for him. We never could get anything in his name. I felt that we were in financial prison; my stress level was always at ten. Communication about this before marriage would have been beneficial.

Another thing to know about insurance, wills, and beneficiaries is that a relative's husband died, and she did not know she was the beneficiary of his policy. The job called and asked if I knew

Mary Stewart, and I did not. They informed me she was the named beneficiary of his policy. This caused problems: the job paid for the funeral, and the named beneficiary never gave the woman or his children a dime.

We should always talk about insurance, housing, cars, how many children, pets, savings, what it costs to run your household, college for the children, the amount needed to contribute, and the amount to save.

We are not to use deception in any way during marriage. When you lie about your finances, it lures you away from God's plan for marriage. Some heads of households think this is being the boss when, in fact, we are partners in our plans. A woman is not below or above her husband but is to enhance and complement the man in every aspect of life. Both should be in every decision when buying a house, car, or investment. Genesis 2:1 states, "God said, "*It was not good for a man to be alone.*" A wife is not just the armpiece or the fulfillment of your desires but also a person of help and support to her husband and family. Many women do not know about the finances and, upon divorce or death, are left in the dark. I read a story where a woman married for many years to her husband did not inherit the house. She had moved into the house that her husband owned. He left the house to his son, her stepson. He allowed her to stay in the house until he married. After more than thirty years of living in the house, she had to find a new place to live. My cousin and his fiancée both had homes but decided to sell them and buy one together. This may be a better way to make sure one is secure in these circumstances and make decisions that the marriage is on one accord—just a suggestion because situations vary in nature.

Where did the idea of divorce come about biblically? It was usually the man's independent work when he was displeased with living with his wife. Traditionally, a woman could not get a divorce. Women were viewed as inferior and had a subordinate position in the marriage. She was primarily the most valued possession of the man. This may be that a dowry was given to the parents, or whoever was responsible for her made her property for the husband.

The Mosaic Law made it hard to get a divorce from a wife. There had to be a trial with a bill of divorcement that had to be within immoral actions, such as adultery. That was not always the case; some men would not be pleased living with their wives for various reasons. A man could not divorce his wife because she gained weight, was a bad cook, or had a personality flaw, only moral acts that would bring shame to the family. Some men would fabricate stories to get the divorce that sometimes did not end well for the woman. Moses advised not to deal treacherously because of the danger it would create. If it is reported that she committed adultery, she could be stoned to death. Women sometimes could not marry again, which she depended on for survival.

Listening to people now, they go into marriage, not anticipating it would last. Now, we have pre-nuptial agreements and situations agreed upon, such as open marriages that practice consensual non-monogamy. You can actually be in a club where you share partners. It is also much easier to get out of the marriage with no-fault divorces, with no one held accountable. If you listen to the news, treachery is as great as the Old Testament. Men killing their wives and children, one killing his pregnant wife, throwing his two children in an oil refinery tank. Another hired a hit man to bludgeon his wife to death, and a woman hired a hit man to kill her husband. Some because they are having an affair, others because they want insurance money, and people who do not wish to be married. Young people are now saying they do not want to get married or have children. 1 Timothy 4:3 states, *"[f]orbidding to marry, and commanding to abstain from foods which God created to be received with thanksgiving by those who believe and know the truth."*

We live in a society where women say they do not need men, and males declare the same. Actually, those who are getting married do so at a later age, as opposed to 20 years, which is 27 years or older. We have so many people not eating meat that it appears to be a religion. I will not go into the meat thing because so much stuff is in food, such as hormones. I understand it.

Divorce is no fun. It is second to death for stress indicators because it feels like someone has died. You go through all the stages of grief. Mental health experts agree that divorce is comparable to the death of a loved one. I went through all the stages of denial, anger, bargaining, depression, and acceptance—the same stages of death. It was devastating when in Christ because marriage is always an analogy of a union that represents the love of God. God says he is married to the backslider and calls the church his bride. One may look at the marriage not just as a human failure, a broken covenant with God. That was my feeling that I disappointed God.

I remember being in denial when someone asked me to join the singles ministry. In my mind, there was no association with being single. When I took off my wedding ring, my heart hurt, and I was angry because I loved the ring and could no longer wear it. The betrayal was overwhelming, but I could not do anything. The sense of loss was overbearing emptiness when you came home from work, eating alone, doing everything alone. Finances are disrupted trying to figure out how to live off one income when you have identical bills. Depression was the worst; I did not want to share with friends or go to events where everyone was married, straight face at work but tears during the night. My time spent eating out, going to the gym, watching movies, and shopping kept me busy. I was getting home at 7 or 8 o'clock just in time to eat and go to bed for two years. I heard a "go home," realizing I had gone through the last stage of acceptance, and my mind felt free for the first time in two years. I accepted being single and was asked by the Pastor to be over the singles ministry.

I also knew that God still loved me, and I was more disappointed than he was. Forgiveness is the key to receiving complete healing, so forgiving my husband and myself was a process and a journey that helped me enter the next chapter of my life with peace.

God has called us to peace if our marriage is plagued with turmoil, drama, and arguments that is not of God.

I mentioned in the beginning that we are to treat each other with the respect that is so often given to people we do not know. Charity begins at home, meaning we should deal with the needs of people close to us before helping others. You pledge love to God and each other, but something blinds that love, and it is the flesh. We fight each other instead of the enemy trying to destroy marriage. Prayer was the key you dismissed when finding people at fault and angry instead of the devil. The Bible says we fight not against flesh and blood. In Ephesians chapter 6, we put on the armor of God to fight against the devil.

We fight for our marriages by focusing on God and his purpose for this union. Do not allow outsiders, such as your mother, father, siblings, or friends, to have input in your marriage. I know mothers who actually talk about their daughter-in-law and criticize everything she does. If your son accepts her, it is none of our business. If she serves dinner at seven and you at six, she thinks she should treat him as if you are wrong. Remember, he left his mother and father to cleave to his wife. Do not take each other for granted, and leave room for changes. Show love and appreciation; there is nothing wrong with saying thank you for cooking my favorite meal or thanks for cleaning my car. Have a time set for romance, dates, prayer, and bible study. Our marriages must be rooted in God; we will not flourish healthily with him.

Doing as the word says is the key to a successful marriage. Ephesians 5:21-23 reads, "*Submitting yourselves one to another in the fear of God.*" Wives, submit yourselves unto your own husbands, as unto the Lord. For the husband is head of the wife, even as Christ is the head of the church and the savior of the body. The one that is never talked about is the husband's love for your wives, even though he loved the church and gave himself for her. (Ep. 5:25). This talks about love for God, love for each other, and mutual respect—not selfishness, but selflessness. It does not mean a woman loses her voice; submission should never be abused or controlled. Let us get this right church and go home.

JEALOUSY IN THE CHURCH

Jealousy is as cruel as the Grave: The coal thereof are coals of fire. (Solomon 8:6)

I never understood why people would have a jealous spirit in the church. God has made each of us unique and beautiful and has given us gifts designed for us. Sometimes, we are unsatisfied with what God has bestowed and lack gratitude and thankfulness for God's gifts. You have to consider that many followers of Christ do not know their purpose or worth in the Kingdom of God. We have the feeling that some callings are more prestigious or better. We should be seeking God to inquire what he wants.

The first recorded incident of jealousy is in Genesis when Cain and Abel give their first fruit as an offering to God. God accepted Abel's offering but not Cain's. Cain was so enraged with jealousy toward his brother that he killed him. He allowed flesh to take control and yield himself to Satan; this changed the trajectory of Cain's path. He had to flee and lived as a fugitive as a marked man for the rest of his life. That is why jealousy is as cruel as the grave. It can cause harm emotionally, physically, and spiritually.

Today, people are seen as threats because of their possessions of talents, gifts, and positions. Some want what others have without knowing the cost the person has made to get what God has given them. Resentment and discontentment with themselves overcome their thinking that they are not enough. I remember a young man teaching and preaching with knowledge and power within a year that people felt being there the longest they should be in his place. Pastor explained that he studied and got before God by fasting and praying. He made sacrifices and was promoted by God, who gave him the increase. We also cannot forget that God is the administrator of all gifts. First Corinthians chapter 12 makes it clear that spiritual gifts are administrated according to God for the church's edification. Chapter 14: 12-13 indicates that not everyone has the same gift.

How do you know when people are jealous of you? I will name a few to help recognize the signs.

They will diminish or not acknowledge your accomplishments. I remember telling a family member that upon getting a promotion as supervisor, she talked about a friend who had received a promotion, talked about the money she made, and told me that she knew people who had my position did not make much. I chalked it up to jealousy, and we spent the rest of the time talking about her friend. Another example is when I purchased a new car and picked up a friend. The car was a week old, and the new car smelled still. She described how a friend had bought an Escalade car, describing its beauty and features. She never acknowledged my car, and it hurt. My personality is such that rejoicing with a family member or friend who receives a blessing is my way of expressing that I am happy for you, and it is genuine. Sometimes, people in a jealous church will never build you up. You delivered a good message or sang a beautiful song, and the house moved to worship; some never say I enjoyed the song or message. Yes, I know we give God the glory, but sometimes we need affirmation that our efforts were good. We should build up our Pastors and leaders, encouraging them to continue.

Talking bad about someone can be an indicator of jealousy. I remember when a supervisor was getting ready to retire, she was mentoring a predecessor. People would go into the office and talk to her about the woman's work, not giving her credit for doing anything good and finding all sorts of faults. The supervisor discerned why people were coming to her about the woman. It was jealousy because a few also had an eye on the job. The church does that, too, going to the Pastor to discourage him from seeing you as who you are. Sometimes, pastors have confidence in people who try to steer their decisions instead of God. We just hope the pastor prayed and heard from God. A person told the pastor that a new couple was not married, an anointed couple, which was not true. The church knows that if they can find something in you, your acceptance in ministry is tarnished. I have heard people say they do not trust him, he used to sell drugs, or he was in prison for thief, she was a prostitute, and he was a pimp. To be honest, we all used to be something. We are new creatures when born-again Christians, according to 1 Corinthians 5:17.

An intimidated church and insecure members can be a sign of jealousy. It is a big problem if pastors and parishioners fear anointed members. They are so afraid they are going to lose their place. You may find yourself sitting in the pews or on the hospitality committee when you can offer more to the ministry. There is nothing wrong with those positions, but they are not specific to you. I have experienced this even in the newborn class at a church. After I finished, the teacher asked how I had served at my former church. I named ministerial staff, praise team, Sunday school teacher, bible study teacher, leader over evangelism, and abstinence classes. The teacher stated in a haughty voice, "You won't be doing any of that here." This shocked me, praying silently, rebuking Satan in Jesus's name. It was nothing new to me because this follows me wherever I go. She was off; God placed me where I belong, on the ministerial staff, choir, and bible study teacher. If people have a problem with what You are blessed to do so; they should take it up with God.

Some people are jealous of anointed brothers and sisters. It is out of Godly character because the person divinely gifted from God is in his rightful place. You cannot obtain it when it does not belong to you. Sometimes, people want your light but do not realize the light is of God. My sister Linda, who was over a sign language and dance ministry, had new people come to the church and wanted to take over. My sister's skills in the area God gave her were enjoyed by many, but for some reason, visiting the church, this woman now was over the ministry; my sister said she just started her own group, and the women that were in my sister's group were now in hers. We have to be careful with this attitude; Lucifer wanted what God had even though the glory was upon him, the best position in the heavenly choir, but wanted something that was not his: God's Kingdom and his glory. Betty wants to sing like Lucy, Robert intends to preach like Paul, and Sandy wants to teach like Jean.

Nevertheless, you cannot obtain something that does not belong to you when it is not your anointing or calling. The woman eventually left the church because she could not walk in obedience to the ministry. When asked by the pastor to make herself and her group available, she said she would not. After a disagreement, she became angry and left the church. Peter 1:10 tells us to make our calling and election sure, for in doing so, you will never stumble. When it is your assignment called to God, it will not fail if you seek Him. Seek your own gift, not others'.

People who are critical of everything could be another sign of jealousy. No one can do anything right. The choir cannot sing, and the church is too little or too big. I was perturbed by a family member complaining about food at my daughter's wedding. She kept saying that she could have cooked the food better. Many told me the food was delicious. Sometimes, people criticize your ideas; they need to change before we use them.

I am so used to giving my ideas taken right from underneath me. One situation recalled is when submitting a cookbook for a fundraiser. It was on hold for another date. A few months later, an announcement was made at a meeting that the cookbook would be a fundraiser for the church named Humble Pie. My name was never mentioned, and the person who would preside over it was revealed. After the meeting, the woman came to me to say she knew it was my idea, but the First Lady wanted her to do it. I did not say a word; I just wished her well. The book never happened, not ever mentioned again. This proves that if something is not for you, it is not for you. My Mother, Lillian Wade, was an excellent cook, and one day, I want to put her recipes in a book. When people are critical, they usually do not give compliments. Sometimes, people will say things as you look like you gained weight. The motive can be questionable if they never say anything good about you, and we need to stay away and choose people who build us up.

Competitive personalities can be a sign of jealousy, as someone is always trying to up one you. You purchase a modest house, and they buy one on the lake. If you change your hair, they will go and get the same hairdo and say they were thinking about getting their hair like that for a long time. When you talk about your family and are so proud of telling them the news of your child getting into medical school, they will not let you finish before they tell you about their children's accomplishments, bigger and greater. You cannot tell your plans either; if you tell that person I am giving the First Lady a dozen roses for her birthday, they will bring two dozen Sunday morning. I remember a pastor saying he was giving a tent revival and told another pastor. The other pastor announced his revival at the same time near the same location as the pastor.

The pastor was in constant competition with that pastor until he moved to another state. My biggest hurt was getting a promotion and sharing it with a family member. She could not compete, so she pitted her friend against me. She talked about her friend's promotion and how much money she was making, mentioning all her degrees. The conversation ended with her saying that a woman she knew had my job and that they do not make much money in those positions. Never give congratulations; I am happy for you, nothing. This was jealousy, and the fact that a family member would feel that way was troublesome—a problem emulation; a person who tries to match or surpass in achievements by imitation. An envious rival could be a girlfriend who looks up to you and wants to copy everything you do. This is annoying because people usually want to be their unique selves without a twin.

The most serious example is a co-worker who confided she loved the supervisor. She moved where he was when he accepted a job in another town. He was engaged to a co-worker, and we were all invited. She arrived late to the wedding just in time for the bride to march down. Instead of going outside the aisle, she walked down the aisle right behind the bride. No one thought it was a mistake at all. She wanted to be Julie. She did not stay for the reception; it had to be very painful. She wrote me a letter saying she would become a nun and wanted my thoughts on it. I suggested that she made sure this was what she wanted to do. I felt she gave up on life. It is sad because when you cannot be someone else, there is nothing wrong with being you. You miss out on what God has for you, living to be like someone else when we are fearfully, wonderfully made, marvelous are thy works, and thy soul know quite well. *"I will praise You, for [a] I am fearfully and wonderfully made; Marvelous are Your works, And that my soul knows very well."* (Psalms 139:14).

Another sign of jealousy is when someone gloats over your mistakes. You confided in Susan that you did not pass the bar, so she called everyone you know.

Friends are encouraging you to get another opportunity. You know Susie put out the news because you told no one else.

Some signs may be people giving you bad advice. It can be about anything from your relationship to a purchase you are about to make. They may tell you that they do not like your *fiancé*, and it may sound like this: He tried to talk to me, but he is too fat for me. What do you see in him? You can do better. You should have stayed with Joe; at least he had a better-paying job. You like the Ford Fusion when sharing about purchases, but the person tells you it is unreliable. I know people who have problems with that car. If you do not buy the car, they wave at you, driving the car you wanted. Many people are not in your best interest if they are jealous. They will say or do anything to block your blessings, but they are blocking theirs. I am firmly in the belief that you reap what you sow. I would rather shop with my daughter, who would be honest and want what is best for me. Never tell people your plans just show up and let them see whatever you possess for the first time. This is something people with good hearts must learn.

Another sign is that people covet what yours. I remember when three women told me I had their job and that I was the token black. The conversation went on to say that I want your job during the day so I can finish school. Can you work nights? I mentioned having two school-age children. My son was in Junior High, and my daughter was in elementary school. These women asked if I wanted some water, and I ended up in the hospital, having seizures and fighting for my life. The doctors said my condition was drug-induced, but I did not take drugs or even medicine.

I was a born-again, and this went against my Christian values. My father said someone on your job gave you something the Lord had shown him. I could not remember because I had lost my memory and was having seizures and a temperature of 104 and 105 they could not get down. They thought I would die due to having inflammation of the brain. Encephalitis was diagnosed, and I felt I would die from the headaches alone. There were so many prayers for me, and I got better. They had once said my life would be like a vegetable. My memory was something that came back slowly. I prayed about if my co-workers had given me something, and the glass of water appeared before me and told my father. I never let anyone bring me drinks, and I never leave the table without a trusted presence when going out to eat.

One of the women quit before I came back; the other stayed and offered to pay my rent. I refused the rent offer, and she left soon after I returned to work elsewhere. You hear it all the time in crime stories: a woman killed her sister because of jealousy to assume her identity. The sister was successful and cared for her sister, who had never done much for herself. She burned the house down, and the sister was unrecognizable, so people thought she was the sister. Someone who knew them recognized she was not who she said she was. The woman got arrested was sentenced to life in prison.

Another is when someone slanders your name. How many people have died because of hurtful words? The tongue can be very divisive and has the power of life or death. Satan can use your tongue to put people down, lie, and complain. Jealousy is very dangerous; that is why the scripture read that it was as cruel as the grave.

One movie in the '60s called *The Children's Hour* tells the story of two teachers who ran a private school. A student made up a story that they were lovers after she was disciplined. The parents removed the children from the school, and they lost their livelihood. The school closed, and one of the teachers took her life.

I know that in this day and age, people would say that it should not be a problem, but it was during that time that this lifestyle was not accepted. This has happened in the church before. As I mentioned earlier, a couple came to our church and said not to be married and to live in adultery. The goal was to kill their influence. The two talented people became the Minister of Music and Choir Director. The devil wanted to stop them in their tracks, but when God has something for you, no one can stop it.

We have to live in the spirit that helps us to walk in the spirit. What happens is that the flesh takes over, not commanded to stay subject to Christ. A friend mentioned jealousy aloud and prayed when it tried her; this made me admire her as an utmost disciplined Christian, putting Satan under her feet—a true example of living and walking in the spirit.

I know that people think highly of themselves and are selfish in society. Philippians 2:3 reads, "*Let nothing be done through strife or vainglory: but in lowliness of mind let each esteem others better than themselves.*" Our best way to defeat the spirit of jealousy is to walk in the spirit so we do not fulfill the lust of the flesh, Galatians 5:16. Regard our brothers and sisters as neighbors; we should love them as ourselves. If we actually lived by this, there would be heaven on earth, no jealousy, no murder, or hate. Remember that you have not been replaced. Just someone got a promotion.

Let's get it right and go home.

GIMMICKS

"God is a Spirit, and they that worship him must worship him in spirit and in truth" (John 4:24).

The late Apostle Henton often stated that God does need the Devil's help. What did he mean by that? Since the church is based on the spirit of Jesus and the spirit of God in holiness, and the devil represents the world's evil, it cannot coincide in the same place. Some older saints do not like new stuff like rap, gospel, dancing, and come as you are. They felt that you need activities for the youth to keep them interested but not compromise with the world. The Washington Post just wrote that millennials want back in the pews and want the church to stop being cool. Rachel Held Evans stated in the article that they are not looking for freshly brewed coffee, heavily bearded worship leaders, and music that sounds like something from the top of the charts. She mentioned that iPads were given away at the end of the service by drawing numbers. Church attendance according to the Forum on Religion and Public Life, 59 percent of young people with church backgrounds ages 18 to 29 is low. The article said that cool bands, hipper worship, edgier programming, and technology are not impressive. We are using so many gimmicks that we are losing the key to what draws people. The millennials appear to want something more meaningful to draw them to God. My father would say that the spirit that draws me also draws young people. He would go on to say there is no old Holy Ghost or young Holy Ghost. We cannot lure people to church with gifts of televisions, tablets, and iPhones. We only need the Holy Spirit and his word, which draws all of us to God. Millennials also prefer a classic church rather than a hip one. I am just learning this, too, and am amazed at it.

People do not want to be entertained but, like the word of God, are filled with strength for the coming days. We have experienced a hard two and a half years with a pandemic, losing jobs, evictions, family and political discourse, and unaffordable living costs for everything. Gas is almost six dollars, and a dozen eggs for four dollars, while housing sometimes rises to a couple thousand dollars more. One young woman interviewed on the news said her rent was $ 1500, raised close to $ 3000 monthly. She would not be able to afford it and was facing homelessness. We are now looking for the good news of the gospel for hope. People need to feel there is a way of peace to help with the stress and pain. Many have lost family members to COVID-19, and people who had the virus are still experiencing symptoms and unable to return to work. Many couples during the pandemic got divorced. It does appear that revival is needed in the church. Young people are not into churches where money and prosperity are more important than spiritual needs.

My parents were distraught with the church they used to attend. They were having a raffle, and the item used was a fifth of whiskey. Many did not agree, but the majority voted for this fundraiser. The crazy thing was that this would appeal to sinners, and membership would go up; emphasis would not be put on soul-winning but on a head count for more offerings. I questioned a member of the church who had no problem with it because he did not think anything was wrong with drinking. My thoughts are that an alcoholic could win and cause all sorts of problems, such as drunk driving. These are people whose minds are not on heavenly things but on the world. Colossians 3:2 read, "*Set your minds on things above, not on earthly thing. For you died and your life is now hidden with Christ in God*". This means that God does not need the Devil's help to build his church. People want something for their souls, not for their bodies.

Raffles have always been a problem because I am not good at selling or asking for money. I was once asked to sell raffles for a concert. Everyone had to sell ten tickets, and the ones not sold came out of your pocket. I refused because being a single parent would not be good for me. After paying all my bills and caring for my children's needs, twenty dollars remained each pay period to catch the bus for work and go to the dollar movie once a month. Something my children looked forward to. I considered being rebellious from that day at the church, but that was ok. Some other people felt the same way and refused too. We had a membership of about four hundred, meaning a profit of forty thousand dollars.

My father told me this story: he was speaking at a conference, and the church pastor took him into the office and offered him whiskey before he spoke, saying he would preach better. The pastor said he did it every time he preached, which helped him. My father told the pastor he allowed the Holy Spirit to help him preach. I must say again that God does not need the Devil's help. What the pastor did not know is that before my father came to Christ, he had an alcohol use disorder. Our home was in turmoil on weekends, with no peace at all. There were arguments all the time because he would tell Mom he had nothing to drink. I took up for my mother at the time, so there was abuse from my dad. I had a busted mouth one day, so my mom had a lawyer to write a letter telling my dad what the consequences could be. He stopped beating me. No one knows what happens in people's homes; it behooves us to be a hindrance for unbelievers or people of God.

The other Gimmick I want to address is something that most people may not see as a problem. At another church, my daughter and I went to hear a famous duo that was popular during the '70s. They shared the gospel and testimonies and sang. At the end of their sharing, they stated that the church should be having fun and had people do the electric slide. Can you believe it, saints dancing and reveling, my daughter and I left vexed; what was the pastor thinking?

Millennials are not going to church to be entertained, but something went down that I would never have imagined. It was bad enough that church members were doing the electric slide on the altar at another church. The youth leader at an apostolic church submitted a plan for a prom, and the pastor approved it. This man stated he had missed his prom, and it seems as though some others had too. Many were on board, but my ex-husband and I were not. Of course, there were others who had been in Pentecostal church all their lives, and dancing was not what they did, even though all dancing is wrong, such as ballet, Indian dances, and many more. It was something the Pentecostal church did not do. Actually, secular music is abandoned for spiritual gospel songs. Some of us could not wrap our heads around sanctified people set aside for God's use and had an appetite for worldly activities such as this. Well, it did happen: tickets were sold, and the venue was acquired.

News circulated that the dance had to stop because of dirty dancing. The pastor instructed that couples should dance only with each other, but that did not happen. I said earlier what this has to do with winning souls. I remember a person at my job invited me to a party, and we talked about what would happen at the party. Alcohol and marijuana would be a part of the festivities. Of course, I could not go. They saw nothing wrong with it as long as I did not engage in that; they just wanted my presence. As we talked, I questioned them if I came after that, could I witness Christ. There was silence, and the answer was "no." That was the conclusion of the whole matter that we should remain witnesses in good standing with God.

Another gimmick is that you have a contest to get a prize for inviting the most people to church. The thing is, there is a head count to earn more money that Sunday. I will not say the motive is only for money, but souls are not on the front burner. Most members brought friends and family that already had church homes. Others came but, in advance, communicated that they were not going to the altar for salvation. One person won a television at Family and Friends day for the most people coming to church that Sunday. No souls were saved, even though the harvest was present.

As a youth, I remember the quarter-gleaning cards; a popular event was getting quarter donations that fit in the slots. There was a prize for whoever collected the most money. You always had the one person, Shirley Jones, who would turn in one to two hundred dollars. Three children in our family participated, but we still got around twenty-five dollars because we knew the same people. This was in the '50s and '60s; if five hundred dollars were raised, that would be good money back in the day. When you became a teen, it stopped; there were no more quarter cards, which was fine with me because I was never good at begging. The prize would be twenty-five dollars, a toy and candy.

The other things were selling dinners and having bake sales. Sometimes, you pay more for the ingredients than your profit. People said they would rather donate if they spent twenty dollars and only made twenty. No dinners sold at the church I go to now; we survive on tithes and offerings as instructed in the bible. My mother's church would have a Heaven and Hell dinner every year. The menu was chili and ice cream. I always chuckled at this because it was fun and odd, but they did pretty well on that. However, the name was disturbing to me. I love chili and did not want it associated with Hell. I just hope no one thinks Hell is no hotter than chili. When I was growing up, tithes were never taught, but I knew about all the dinners, bake sales, and raffles. Churches do not realize you burn out your members that way. The millennials stated they did not want to be concerned about money schemes but were willing to support the church financially.

God's house is to sustain itself on tithes and offerings according to Malachi 3:10 and Psalms 3:8-10. "Honor the Lord with your possessions with the first fruit of all your increase; so your barns will be filled with plenty, and vats will overflow with new wine. They want to give without gimmicks or threats that your car will stop running, or your child may get sick, and your marriage may fail. Yes, I have heard all of this. Leaders have to repent because it is not scripture. They never quote the scripture that says not to give begrudgingly or out of necessity. One mother of the church asked me if she should give tithes or buy her medicine. She did not have enough money to do both, so I advised her to purchase her medication. I remember a friend telling me her husband had recently been laid off, and she was taking care of all the bills. I suggested she still pay her tithes because that is what my pastor told me when that happened to my ex-husband. She answered, "No." I talked to my pastor about it and stated that she gives according to her ability. My friend said that when he returns to work, she will start at that point and ask God for forgiveness. This was my first time hearing someone asking God for forgiveness for not being able to give as she once did. It was not as if she was buying new clothes, electronics, and luxury items. It says in Malachi, 3:9 that you are curse with a curse for ye have robbed me, even this whole nation. The Bible says he will show kindness to whom he shows kindness and mercy to whom he shows mercy. God forgives whom he pleases; his mercy endures forever. A pastor once said he was looking at shoes to judge whether they were new if you were not tithing. Let God judge this; I am glad he is not God. Pastors do not realize how they turn so many away by making people feel guilty. Some people have expressed this as why they do not attend church.

We do not want contests in the church because that is not edifying. I am not saying you cannot have a church picnic or sack race. Most people wish for churches to have activities to bring the body together with family and friends.

Church let soul winning be our priority and quit the entertainment. Let us return to the old landmark, our first love of God's work to help fill his kingdom. Invite the Holy Spirit in. I guarantee you that the presence of God is better than any experience you can have. Go back to prayer, fasting, and the true worship of God. Get it right, go to church, and prepare to go home.

Sexual Sin 2

"Flee sexual immorality. Every sin that a man does is outside the body, but he who commits sexual immorality sins against his own body." (1 Corinthians 6:18).

I like using the New King James Version for my scripture in this chapter because it explains it with slightly different wording. King James's version says, "Flee fornication." Some may think they are just talking about unmarried people, but the latter seems more evident that all sexual sin is immorality. The only sexual union God recognizes is the coupling of male and female in marriage. The Lord God made man first and said it was not good for him to be alone; I will make him a helpmeet.

God put Adam in a deep sleep, took the rib from man, and created woman. All the pronouns in Genesis are he, she, him, man, and woman, referring to the man and the woman. This pertained to a man and woman, not any other alternate beings that are not of God but man-made. God does not go against Himself; to say anything else, you are making God a liar, and he cannot lie. (Hebrews 6:18). People will use God's not exist argument because they think this is a way not to acknowledge or obey him. Well, sorry, God is not going to take His word back. I am so sick of sexual sin in the church, a situation that caused me to move my membership to another fellowship.

I felt betrayed beyond betrayal. My emotional state was on the brink because my pastor touched me. It was not what I saw but felt. It was confusing; he was coming down the outer aisle where he taps people on the shoulder or shake hands as he leaves after his sermon. My head was down, and my eyes were closed upon the benediction as requested by the minister presiding. I felt a touch on my backside and looked up as he was passing. I went home and prayed because it was creepy. Something said in my heart: you will be hated as Tamar. I knew the story from 2 Samuel 13, where Amnon raped his half-sister and afterward despised her.

The next day, during Sunday school, the pastor attended. This was different because the five years as a member never saw him in the class. He sat across from me and never said a word; he just looked at me contemptuously. I had not spoken to anyone but asked the person sitting why the pastor was looking our way. She said she did not know. I felt so uncomfortable, and it all came out when he began speaking from the pulpit. He started by saying people at the church had lied to him in the past, and if anyone says he touched them, it is a lie. Everything came together, knowing that this would be my last day; this caused me much pain. I did not know exactly what to do. I went to church the next week, thinking it was in my mind and it would go away. I asked to play a part in the women's ministry. I would be over prayer. I was summoned to the front of the church near him, and he gave me that look again. I felt he was trying to intimidate me. That was my last day as a member. I immediately called my sister Beverly, told her everything, and talked to her husband, Pastor Miller, about moving membership under his leadership. He was someone I trusted and looked up too. He has always been transparent and true to the work of God. No scandals surround him in any area of his life, marital or spiritual matters of the church. This would be the place to feel protected and loved. My days were hard after that. I slept in a fetal position and cried for weeks. I was emotionally drained because every hurt from all the men in my past surfaced. I thought about the betrayal of affairs by my children's father, my first husband, and the lack of honesty and integrity from my second husband. The history of molestation by our neighbor at the age of eight haunted me, too. My emotions were all over the place to the point of feeling God was so far away that he did not hear or care for me anymore. I was numb and tried to share with a few people I felt were not in my corner. Many people today still will take up for these men. Famous saying, we do not believe he will do such a thing. Jeremiah 17: 9-10 states, *"The heart is deceitful above all things, and desperately wicked; who can know it. The Lord searches the heart; test the mind, even to give every man according to his ways, according to the fruit of his doings."* I always think of this scripture when people appear surprised by someone's evil actions.

There are a few situations that came to mind: a childhood friend who had an affair with a pastor of the church my family once attended, a pastor who impregnated a young member, leaving his wife to marry her, and a pastor who had an affair where the woman and child belong to the church, his wife was Assistant Pastor.

My friend Karen had a sister, Betty, and my sister Linda and I were close too. We lived in the same neighborhood. It was a unique community in that most families had the same values. The love for God, family, and neighbors was vital in those days; in the '50s and '60s, people seemed closer and looked out for one another. People had moral values, and there were things you did not do. We had rules to respect our elders and everyone, and you did not take anything that did not belong to you. This was when families went to church, ate, and watched Ed Sullivan and Gun Smoke. If your boyfriend was present, he sat in the same room with the family. You get what I mean.

Sex is everywhere: television, commercials, advertisements, music, and fashion; nothing is sold without it. A commercial for hot dogs was taken off the air by the public's demand because it implied the man was promoting his private part by sultry saying, "I have a hot dog for you." A beautiful woman is on the beach in a bikini that he approaches. The message that was to be subliminal was not at all. Why do women have to be scantily clad to sell a car or furniture or eat a strawberry seductively is crazy. I remember a known movie star on a talk show said in her five-year-old voice she wanted to be sexy. The mother was afraid of what her child thought about what was sexy. Actually, she found out that her daughter wanted to dress like mommy. There is a problem when parents allow their children to dress older with crop tops, dresses, blouses off the shoulder, and short shorts. Some of these children are toddlers and young children; parents think it is cute, but it violates making sure your child can live out their childhood lives as a child. There are too many crazies in the world to expose them in this manner.

Women are not innocent in the seductive sexual mongering causing trouble in the church. I have seen women with skirts up to their vagina, tops showing cleavage and almost nipples, see through clothes without undergarments. They have makeup on thick lashes that are an inch long. Are they going to the club or church? We go to church for one thing only: to worship God and honor his word. The star should only be God. All other distractions are out of order. I went to church very appropriately and witnessed glares of disrobing, so unconvertable I kept holding my head down. This is a person in the pulpit with views of all of us. He said he liked looking at women. That was a weakness. He rather says it is a weakness than a spirit of lust because that is exactly what is running rampant in the church. There are so many stories, but I will only tell a few because these issues drain me.

I was walking on campus toward my bank when a female student paced her walk beside me. We engaged in conversation, and if I recall correctly, she asked me if I was looking for a job. She stated that her job was at the local bank downtown. I told her I had a job and that working at a bank would not be my thing. She seemed quite friendly; we ended up going to a pizzeria on campus before our next classes. We exchanged phone numbers and went our separate ways. We talked on the phone, sharing being a single parent of two children and her life living on campus. I shared that I was born-again and went to church on campus. She stated she was also a Christian but not familiar with the church held in the auditorium of Illinois State University. Sharon wanted to go to church with me, and we made plans for her to attend the next meeting. She came and enjoyed the services. Our communication was Sharon calling me. I was busy with my children, school, and work, so initiating calls hardly happened. This being in the '70s, no one had a cell phone. How did we ever make it? Interesting. You made do with what you had access to, and telephone booths were near every block.

There was a night we talked about Sharon having a boyfriend and that he was a pastor; she wanted me to meet him. She said he was a young man and a Methodist pastor. We arranged for me to meet him, and a man I knew from Danville, Illinois, was with him. I was glad to see Carl Roberts because we both served on the Student

Council at Danville Junior College. He wanted to date me, but I was never attracted to him. He tricked me on a date and disguised it as a formal council meeting at a nice restaurant in the Raddison Hotel. The plan was to wear after five attire. We arrived at 7 pm, and at 7:45 pm, no one had come yet; five others were to join us. It turned out he tricked me and told me there was no meeting; this was the only way he could take me to dinner. I never thought much of him after that. As I looked at these two men, they reminded me of slender man. I am not kidding. The Pastor wore a black suit, trench coat, shoes, and one of those top hats that clergy wear. Carl wore regular clothes, a plaid shirt, and jeans, a casual, slender man. They were both slightly built and ghostly-looking; they said they had just arrived at a leadership conference. I found nothing to draw a young woman about 19 years of age to him. He looked like a minister depicting the 1800s in that all-black attire. Sharon was attractive and petite, with a short pixie haircut like Holly Berry's, smooth brown skin, and big brown eyes. She could do a lot better. I was not impressed. He looked in his early thirties, and I wondered if a wife existed. We talked a little weather talk, and then they left. Sharon was gloating, so happy she said she would call me.

Sharon called that night and spilled the beans about this relationship. She stated he was married but said he had no relationship with his wife; they slept in separate beds and were going to separate before he was transferred to Moline, Illinois. She went on to say the Lord had told her he was her husband. I retorted that God does not go against Himself and is not the author of confusion. Why would God give you somebody else's husband when it says, "Do not commit adultery," seventh of the Ten Commandments? I went on to say that the classic stories of men who cheat are that they do not have intimacy with their wives and will go as far as she does not cook or clean. She hung up on me.

I know this all so well because before, my life in Christ was caught in some mess like this. He said his wife had left him, but found out the woman was away in college trying to make up because she was on academic probation at another college. He said all the things that most men say about their wives when having an affair.

Then something came to me: They planned to use my apartment as a meeting place. The Methodist pastor assigned to Moline, Illinois, took his wife and two small children. I saw Sharon on campus; she rolled her eyes at me and did not speak. I never heard from her again.

The next story is so bizarre and scandalous that I still do not believe this happened. My ex-husband and I were looking for a church home. We had not made a choice but had the opportunity to hear a dynamic minister and wanted to listen to him again. One Sunday, we decided to visit the church; it had a wonderful choir, and the preaching was so good. We went about three times before we became members. The people were so friendly and welcoming, and they made us feel at home. I always felt that fellowship with other believers in Christ is joyous. Since both of us ministered, we were put on the roster. I joined the choir, which I have always enjoyed because my family sang as a group for many years in our hometown of Danville, Illinois. We also have a CD out of which my brother wrote the songs. We immediately became active and felt good about moving to this church.

The unique thing is that it's a Baptist church, a charismatic assembly that speaks in tongues and lays hands on the sick. This was what we were used to. However, this was my weakness and misunderstanding. I felt that even though one might err or have sin in their lives, deliverance always sought to be in obedience. Speaking in tongues was for people who stood above the rest in life for Christ, gifts of the spirit, and healing.

Boy, I was in for a rude awakening. The pastor's wife asked if I would go to lunch with her after church to get to know me. I was excited. She was beautiful and tall with a dark complexion and bouncing hair. Her dress was always stylish, and she wore things I never saw in the stores. Her face was boyish but soft. I loved her hair. When she walked, it moved with her, making her look graceful if such a thing.

I thought we would go as a couple with her husband and mine; maybe this is what she does with all new female members. I let my husband know of the plan, and he was okay and would pick up something to eat. It was easy to share information about our children, five for her, me, and two. We discussed our spiritual journey and what we had done in ministry.

We began to talk on the phone daily. I found out she had a radio program at 10 am every morning. She was an evangelist and sang like an angel. I kept thinking how blessed she and the pastor were. He always acknowledges her during the benediction, calling her up to stand beside him, calling her his beautiful wife. It is always something to note when a leader shows endearing actions toward his wife. I remember a preacher saying that if a minister is up talking, look at his wife's expressions. You can tell if things are right at home according to how she responds. I never saw anything that was not positive when they were up speaking.

One day, she asked me to be her prayer partner, saying she loved my spirit and appeared to be a woman of God. Praying that morning speaking that her husband seems far away, where is your husband? When the prayer was finished, she said, "You are a real woman of God because I don't know where my husband is." He had not been home for two to three months, and she did not know where he lived. I was so confused, questioning her about them seeming together on Sundays. I felt betrayed and told her so.

It was time to share this with my husband; he did not appear to be surprised; his attitude was, oh well. This would rattle his brain; he hated situations like this in the church. We knew too many stories of infidelities and affairs in the church. The former church before we moved to the suburbs involved a story of a deacon who had impregnated a student. The sad thing was that he was at her home to give comfort after her mother's death. He was also newlywed with a new baby. We had a meeting where this young woman said to be a Jezebel and a home wrecker. The deacon was praised and encouraged as if he had done nothing. We left the church soon after that. The story has it that the couple miraculously stayed together, and he denied the child who looked like his twin. The young woman was distraught and left the church. Her story was that she was at her most vulnerable time due to grieving her mother's death, and she had the encounter with the deacon.

We knew that our time was going to be short there, but it was not until Pastor Cole called a meeting with me. There were three people in the meeting: two deacons and Evangelist Green. He informed me that he did not leave his wife because he had a girlfriend but because his wife spoke badly to the congregants. The deacons and evangelists were shaking their eyes in agreement. I did not say a word because I had never seen him with anyone, but the woman was the secretary. They had a daughter who was sixteen years old. I still remember when she was led to the vestibule as the other children presented him with a gift for his birthday. She had been sitting with them, happy, smiling, before being asked to leave. I looked out, and the girl was sobbing. My heart was pained. How could they do this to a child? I found out later that he was living with them, not with his wife. As I write this, my emotions are going back there. We left after that. They married and bought a church in my neighborhood about a month ago. I received a notification about the opening as everyone in this building. I actually wanted to be noisy but heard the spirit say not to step foot in that church.

This next story is really heartbreaking because a minister, bishop, and teacher became one of the biggest disappointments in my Christian walk. Many listen to him on Saturday night for the Sunday school lesson. Sunday school lessons are universal or designed for a certain Christian assembly, helping the church to be on one accord. He was the best of the best. His voice was gentle and raspy, and he was a seasoned teacher. I taught Sunday school, which gave me a different view of the lesson. You know, the ones that can skillfully handle the word of God and break it down for everyone to understand. He would find nuggets of knowledge that others may not have gotten.

Anointed to teach, preach, and lead God's people at the time, many aborted the calling. I remember my pastor yielding the floor to him, calling him the greatest preacher in the world. I found this disturbing because my pastor was the speaker for the night. His presence was intimidating because of his charismatic personality and preaching skills. His presence demanded respect, as he was a tall, large man, reminding me of Thurgood Marshall, a nice-looking man with a beautiful and anointed wife. She could sing and evangelize.

The news was out that he had gotten a young woman pregnant his daughter's age and had left his wife for her. Everyone was talking; I knew it was true when a female pastor that I was close to stated she held his wife in her arms and rocked her as she cried. The report was that the evangelist was very broken and pitiful. She is so beautiful and classy, tall, poised, and elegant. The Bishop was leaving her for a twenty-something-year-old his daughter's age.

You know when David said his foot almost slipped when he saw the prosperity of the wicked Psalms 73: 2-3. This seemingly successful man had fallen, making others question if we should stay in the fight. I think what got me, as mentioned before, was that people who possessed gifts in ministry made me feel they were among the best of us. They would have arrived in God with great faith and righteousness if they spoke in tongues. I know my walk is real, but you can be strong and think this threatens the gospel and stability of faith. This was not the first time scandals had been heard in the church, but this one hit harder. Scriptures came to me that we are to look or trust no man. Psalms 146 reads, *"Do not put your trust in prince, mortal men, who cannot save."* It goes on to say that when their spirits depart, they return to the ground with no more plans but the Lord, who remains faithful forever.

Knowing this, I had to get a grip and keep my mind on God to have peace. That is what we have to do to finish the course, filling ourselves with God's word. James 1:12 says, *"Blessed is he that endures temptation for when he is tried, he shall receive the crown of life, which the Lord hath promise to them that love him.*" Paul stated he was pressing toward the mark of the high calling of Christ. We cannot jeopardize our walk with God for a moment of pleasure. Remember, the devil will send people who look good, smell good, talk good, and become the angel of light.

Women are sometimes weak to the deception of wanting something not designed for them. How does one go to a church and claim the pastor as a husband? Talking about the devil going to church makes this a prime example. There is a lot of talk about men, but it takes two to get tangled up. Women, be mindful of waiting on God and not trying to do it yourselves. Go to church to get the fullness of God, not a man. *"First seek God and his righteousness, and all things will be added to you"* (Matthew 5:33). We seek God to have a relationship and protection, but we are responsible for mortifying the deeds of our flesh and resisting the devil that he flees.

We entertain thoughts and situations that we should not, allowing Satan to get a foothold in our lives. Lust comes to the mind first, and it gets stronger as we let it grow in intensity. I remember a pastor saying that if you do not feed it, it will die. The word says that if you look at a married person in lust, you have already committed adultery. We cannot feed on everything presented to us: money, material goods, and people because everything that looks good is not always good for us.

In a cautionary story, a minister involved in an affair, when accused, said that it was not true. The woman had given him an alternative to leave his wife. He did not leave, so she invited him to a hotel and put his pictures on the internet naked. It was not good for this man, the talk of the church. As Paul said, let this behavior not be named among you. 1 Corinthians 7: 1-2 reads, *"It is good for man not to touch a woman. Nevertheless, to avoid fornication, let every man have his own wife, and every woman have her own husband."* God has an order for man when it comes to relationships. People have found out someone is their half-sister or cousin upon dating. My father always told his daughters that if they have a baby, they should not use his last name but the father's due to confusion. Let us get this sin out of our churches, repent, and go home.

YOU CAN'T CATCH
THE HOLY GHOST

"But ye shall receive power after that the Holy Ghost is come upon you: and ye shall be witnesses unto me both in Jerusalem, and in all Judaea, and Samaria, and the uttermost part of the world" (Acts 1:8).

This is going to be short and sweet, but I have to put the impression of the Holy Ghost in perspective. I have often heard the phrase: did you see them catch the Holy Ghost? Usually, they talk about someone shouting, yelling, or jumping when the music is playing. People will say you sure did see the Holy Ghost today, like catching a ball, a cold, or a taxicab. Some people say to hail a cab, but we say to catch a cab in the Midwest. That is crazy, too, because it sounds like we are in the street running to get service.

Have you ever attended a church where you felt the minister was unsatisfied with the service? The choir had a song, fervent prayer went forth, and the pastor preached a good message, but you were asked to stand up, turn around three times, jump, and run around the church, trying to get an emotional reaction. That is what it is: emotions; the spirit of God has left the room, and now you are acting out of flesh because you do not think God has done enough. God has done more than enough, so why are we trying to behave like God? This shows you there is no understanding of the Spirit of God and how he moves. No wonder people are saying you caught the Holy Ghost.

I went to a church when I was younger where the Holy Ghost was never mentioned, and after a while, I realized they associated it with speaking in tongues. Some churches that teach about the spirit of God are lacking and so misunderstood. So what is the Holy Ghost?

The Holy Ghost is the third person of the Godhead. He is the Holy Spirit of God, the Spirit of the Lord, or the Comforter. What is the purpose of the Holy Ghost?

A witness for God's Kingdom Acts 1:8, "But ye shall receive power after the Holy Ghost comes upon you: and ye shall be witness unto me both in all Judea, and in Samaria and the uttermost part of the earth." This is the great commission to evangelize the good news of Jesus and witness salvation to those on the earth. That God has raised Jesus from the dead for the remission of sin. He has given us the power to inform us that Jesus is the Son of God, and he will raise us from the dead to live eternally with him.

To comfort His Disciples, in John 14:16, Jesus says, "I will pray to the Father and he shall give you another Comforter; that he may abide with you forever." The Holy Spirit will be another like Jesus who will advocate for our help in times of trouble. In John 14:18, Jesus says, "I will not leave you comfortless; I will come to you." Jesus knows that going back to his Father leaves us helpless without the help of the Holy Spirit. When Jesus was with his disciples, he was walking and talking Holy Ghost. We need his spirit. I feel like getting up and shouting Hallelujah.

The Holy Ghost teaches you. In John 14:26, Jesus says, "The Comforter which is the Holy Ghost whom the Father will send in my name, he shall teach you all things, and bring things to your remembrance whatever I have said unto you." What he brings to your memory is the word of God. That is why we must study the word of God hidden in our hearts so that it can come to our memory. I remember witnessing to my brother the plan of salvation and God's word of mouth from Genesis to the cross. It was not me but the Spirit of God speaking through me. I remember when God has done this on many occasions. One of the most amazing times was when my co-worker turned off a religious program I had on before he showed up. The minister was talking about alternate lifestyles, not those of God. He asked what I thought about it, and I said I will not give you my opinion but the word of God. The word says we should have a word for all men, and I did from the Holy Spirit. That man and I respected each other until the day I left the job. He understood I was not judging him for his lifestyle but loved him. Pope Francis just said homosexuality was not a crime but a sin and that God only honors marriage as male and female. World listen.

"He shall give you Power to not only witness but to preach the gospel, cast out devils, speak in new tongues, lay hands on the sick that they recover, take of any deadly thing it will not harm you" (Mark 16: 15-18).

You see, the Holy Ghost is not just for you to dance, sing, and roll under pews but to do the work God has commissioned us to do. Phillip the Apostle is a good example of how the Holy Spirit works. An angel of the Lord told Phillip to rise and go south to the road from Jerusalem to Gaza. Phillip saw an Ethiopian eunuch going to Jerusalem to worship. The eunuch seated in his chariot reading the prophet Isaiah. The Spirit told Phillip to go over and join the chariot; he was obedient. He came to him and heard him reading, asking if he knew what; he replied that he did not know whom the Prophet Isaiah was talking about. Phillip begins to tell the eunuch about the good news of Jesus Christ. They passed by water, and the eunuch asked them to be baptized as followers of Jesus. The Bible says the eunuch and Phillip left and never saw each other again. Phillip continued to spread the good news, being obedient to the Holy Spirit to win souls for the Kingdom.

A recent trend started on a game show where a woman begins to chant, "Holy Spirit Activate," to receive the correct words to get points. Immediately, it was all over social media, and everyone chanting it for everything. It is not a trend that can be activated on a whim, but the power of God.

The Holy Ghost convicts us of sin. John 16:7-8 says that he would send us a comforter, and when he comes, he will convict the world of sin and righteousness. Have you heard that voice before your error prompted you not to do it? God's voice is not loud but will tell you not to tell someone off. However, sometimes, we do not listen and find ourselves in a situation where we wish to take back every word. You know, before taking that woman or man home, not yielding to God's voice caused you to commit fornication or adultery. We end up in places not intended for us, and the spirit of conviction leads us not to proceed but repent, never to enter into that sin again. God took out that stony heart and put it in a heart of flesh to receive his spirit and view sin as he sees it. We need the Holy Ghost to lead us to righteousness.

The Holy Ghost gives believers gifts. Gifts of wisdom, knowledge, faith, healing, miracles, prophesy, discernment of spirits, gift of tongues. 1 Corinthians 12:4 reads, "There are diversities of gifts, but the same Spirit. There are different administrations, but they are all the same, Lord. These gifts are to edify the church, build up, and encourage believers. Ephesians 4:13 reads, "That he gave some prophets, evangelists, teachers, pastors for the perfecting of the saints and for the work of the ministry for edifying the body of Christ." It sounds like there is room for every gift. Let us not covet others and seek God for our own. Let us get this right and go home.

MEN LOVE YOUR WIVES WOMEN LOVE YOUR MEN

"Submit to one another out of reverence for Christ."
(Ephesians 5:21).

I am starting with this scripture because it addresses both submissions to Christ. Pastors usually do not mention this or the one that says men should love their wives as Christ loves the Church. The scripture you hear the most is that wives submit to their husbands in all things and submit to their own husbands. Submission needs explanation, or it ends up sometimes being used by abusive authority, which is not God's intention. Submitting to God and each other keeps life in order. Does it mean a woman does not have a voice due to submission? Does it mean she better have my food on the table and my house clean when I return home? Most women would not have a problem if men submitted to God and allowed his direction to come from him. It is our nature to be the softest nurturers who want to please. God. Men are the designated leaders, and no one denies that, but they have to align with God's word to lead. Most women want a strong man who is obedient to God if she is a Christian wife. A man wants a woman who allows him to lead, and that is sometimes a problem.

I talked to teacher Linda Lucas and gave her a take on submission. She says women are afraid to submit to men due to the lack of teaching and what it actually means to men. Men need to be taught what it means to support women who are willing to submit. Women must understand what it means to submit to and support their husbands. There are various ways that submission is viewed.

God did not intend submission to be an abusive authority where you are the boss and directing your mate as if she were a child. There is a saying that you must pay the cost to be the boss. The price is being before God to inquire how you are to lead your family.

Pastor Rodney said that without God, there is no submission from women. He said that without God, your actions come from the flesh. He said that a man is not the boss because God is Lord over us all. That is enough reason to submit because God knows all about us and what we need.

A man is to love, protect, provide, encourage, and allow his wife to have a voice. The two should make decisions on where to live, the car, and raising the children. I remember that when engaged, my fiancé said we no longer would use the soap I used because he only used a certain brand. I asked if we could both use the soap of our choice because we were not able to use the brand he used. He tried to do that in situations, saying we would do this or that without my input. I understood that he did not know this does not work in marriage. You have taken her voice away if she is not helping with decisions.

I asked Pastor Rodney why loving your wife as Christ loved the church is not taught, only submission from the wife. He stated it is because men want to dominate women. Getting him to explain, it seemed as though men viewed treating their wives with the whole love of Christ would make a man look weak. The truth is that they do not want to be obedient to God's word or humble themselves to what would solve misaligned problems in the marriage. Ego is the situation and terrible attribute for anyone; it means you edge God out to work in your power. God gave man a secret in the anecdote to cultivate submissiveness in a wife. Do you know that God knows more? He ordained marriage and designed what works.

One minister says the Bible says wives submit themselves to their husbands, so why do we stop at that? He said a woman wants her husband to lead if he loves as Christ says. She is looking for a responsible husband who provides, protects, loves, is respectful, and listens. There is nothing like having a man that listens to God and his helpmeet. Women should listen to God and their husbands' leads. We cannot stop at one scripture that gives instruction on marriage. Ephesians 5:25 reads, "*Wives submit yourselves unto your own husbands as unto the Lord.*" This is interesting because it says that she should submit to her own husband, meaning she is not accountable to every man. I remember when Bishop Harold Dawson said do not go home to your husband and say the pastor said this or that, causing division in your home, especially if he was not a member of that body of believers. One pastor said if you have a husband who does not agree to give his money to the church, do not give. I know this will work a nerve in some women who make their own money and think he should not say a word about it. Some men think of it as you giving money to another man. I heard a man say he is not going to buy a Cadillac with my money. This is hard, and some pastors have said that if he does not want you to go to church, you should stay home.

Maybe we should see what submission means. Solomon Buchi's article "*The Christian View Of Submission In Marriage Is It A Woman's Call To Slavery*"? Submission means to put yourself under for servicing and supporting your partner. His Greek word for submission was translated as *hupotasso*, which means to get under, lift up, and put in order. Buchi expressed that the biblical concept does not condone subjugation or a woman giving up her will but willfully deploying herself in service to their partner.

A woman should respect her husband, encourage him, and support his dreams and goals; he should be able to do the same.

From my experience, I see it differently concerning the practical works of the scripture for women to subject themselves to their husbands. I hear men say they do not want their wives to work or go to school, and I hear women say I am not cooking, cleaning, or working. I hear men say I am the boss of my house and the King of my castle, but no one can tell me what to do. I have even heard women say this is my house, and he cannot tell me what to do. Men say I work and bring home the bread, so everything is mine. Do you view any submission or humbleness in these statements? No, because selflessness is not submission or display of benevolence or love. The Christian marriage is built on love and far for the desire to control. A person who is controlling is a person who is acting out of fear to feel safe and to feel they have to have things done in their order.

Sometimes, a man or woman thinks things are not done their way and loses control. I know of a story where an older man married a younger woman, a teenager, and had rules that she could not bathe or go outside without him when he went to work. He would check on her when he got home. He was afraid she would meet someone else. She could only go out with a home visitor who worked with teenage mothers. This is not the submission the bible is talking about; God never approves of abusive authority, taking away a person's rights and freedom to move freely. Watching a popular judge program, I saw an episode where a husband took his wife to court to give him at least 100 dollars a week out of his paycheck. He earned 2000 dollars a week, but she felt he did not need it. She stated she fixed his lunch daily, paid the bills, and cared for the house so he had no need for more than 20 dollars a week. He explained to the judge that he would like to have lunch with his co-workers sometimes and would like money to buy her gift instead of asking her for money for her gift. She stuck to that, but the judge awarded him 200 dollars weekly. This wife wanted to control the finances, limiting the husband's decisions. God never wanted spouses to control one another but to love one another with benevolence and respect.

I actually viewed submission, respect, benevolence, and love in a series of couples buying houses. The couples will describe what they want: three bedrooms, two bathrooms, a screened-in porch, and an oceanfront view. In one of the episodes, there was an outhouse with no indoor plumbing; the wife said he could live like that, but that is not for me. The husband insisted she would be just fine. The wife did not argue with her husband but shrugged her shoulders. Another show had an indoor toilet and running water, even though he liked the other house better because they provided him a place to hunt and fish. She wanted him to be happy and asked what he thought was best. He had been adamant at first but concluded that it would not be fair to his wife not to have running water. He knew he probably would not have a clean house or meals with the first house. Oh yeah, there may be bears near the outhouse as well.

This showed them both submitting; the wife was prepared to accept his decision, and the husband understood that for his wife to be happy, she had certain needs. For me, he would have just moved alone and not done an outhouse.

Sometimes, men would call their friends henpecked when they catered or listened to a woman as the word says for a woman to submit to her husband and so the husband the same. We should not allow outsiders to influence our marriages.

It would be a marriage in heaven if a man loved his wife as Christ loved the church. What does that mean? It means he loves her as he loves himself, protects her, and cherishes her as Christ loves the Church. (Ephesians 5:33). He prioritizes her and the relationship. Christ laid his life down for the Church, so a man should be able to do the same. He would never put her in front of him, and as a wild animal approach to shield himself, he would protect her and give her the last piece of bread. He would not provide and depend on her to be the provider or carry the weight of fending for the home. She can help her husband because she is his helpmeet in any area they are agreeable. Believe me, a Christian woman would want to cook, clean, respect, and be affectionate and intimate with this man. Please, woman, accept this type of love and leadership because some still take his kindness as a weakness.

Men keep your business in order and take care of your credit; never allow her name on everything where collectors call. This has happened, and your wife will soon disrespect you and not see you as a leader. Start working on yourself before marriage; let God prepare you for the task. She will never feel protected by you or secure if you cannot handle business. Likewise, a man does not want a wife to be reckless with their affairs. I have known women who spend money and use credit cards to the point that they put their finances in trouble and feel entitled because he took me as a wife.

Make sure that prayer is the most important thing in your marriage. You must come together often because the devil hates this union, and you are building a strong defense against his works. The Bible says two is better than one because he has someone to pick him up when one falls. (Ecclesiastes 4:8-12). We have to remember Satan hates this union, and sometimes, couples fight each other as though they were enemies. When there is division, the ammunition you need to fight the real enemy weakens. I remember saying to my ex that he was acting like the devil, and he would say the same about me. We would get so angry that the flesh would rule. I wished we prayed more than we fought and saw the Devil for who he is. I will say stay in your prayer room. Do not be tricked by the wiles of the Devil. God knows when things align with him and will honor that, and Satan will not win and destroy your marriage.

You are to hold and build each other up because we get weary and down in life's journey. It is not a honeymoon; forever, life happens, and the stress of everything we deal with in the world is not so easy. In the wedding vows, it says I take you as my lawful spouse, to have and to hold from this day forward, for better for worse, for richer, for poorer, in sickness and in health, until death do us part. I will love and honor you all the days of my life. The vows are not in the Bible but based on biblical principles. I want to dwell on the "I will love and honor you all the days of my life." Amazingly, our vows uphold love, respect, and support, building each other until death. When your wife cooks a good meal, is it taken for granted, or do you say thank you that was tasty food? If your husband assembles your bookcase, do you say thank you? Good job, I appreciate you. Do you celebrate accomplishments, and are you there to assist? A Mother's Day and a Father's Day can be special even though we know that she is not your mother or he is father. Getting your children prepared to honor them is your job. You may have to buy the card and the gift when they are young, but you are teaching them how to appreciate someone who does so much to make their lives safe and secure. I remember when my husband was not into giving gifts, but he started doing the same when he received things. It could be something as simple as his favorite dessert or a gift card for a manicure.

My sister and I talked to our nieces about podcasts and social media with panels of men discussing modern women not committing. She is going to cook, clean, serve, have my babies and obey. They did not say she could not work to support him. Worldly men do not really understand the principle of submitting biblically. They seemed to want a woman who was not a partner but someone who would not challenge them to do what they wanted.

A minister teaching on marriage said there were things that men could do to make the relationship better by treating their wife as they treat themselves. (1 Peter 3:7). God did not make man stronger to demean or crush but to love, protect, and honor.

He can make it better by fearing God and keeping his commandment not to give to lust but to give your lives to God. Another principle is being accountable for treating your wife right. Pastors, deacons, and church leaders should address being Christ-like in marriage. I remember pastors telling women to stay with men who beat them and have extramarital affairs. All members of the family have to protect children and can be in the custody of the state for domestic violence, which I have witnessed.

Marriage is an institution of how we have a relationship with God, submitted, obedient, and reverent. We are the Brides of Christ, who is declared Head of the church (Ephesians 5:22-23). Through his death and resurrection, he became a bridegroom and a faithful husband willing to lay down his life for us. The earthly husband is to be the same as the wife, giving his life because of his love.

Let us work on this church; Jesus is coming back; get our house in order and be ready to go home.

DISCIPLINE OUR CHILDREN

"Train up a Child in the way he should go, and when he is old he will not depart from it." (Proverbs 6:22).

Many people are questioning the difference between today's children and those of yesterday when life was more challenging in the past. I remember using the wringer washer, hanging out clothes, ironing, cooking, caring for siblings, and keeping the house clean. Families did things together; we ate together for all three meals. The most important thing was going to church as a family. Our household was based on Christian faith, and the family unit worked peacefully.

We had rules followed without questions because, in my day, there was a saying that children are to be seen but not heard; we could not be in the same room where adults were talking. We could not talk back to our parents, respect elders, come home on time, do chores, no fights or gossip. We bathed daily and wore clean clothes and socks. One I must not miss is that we could not enter a neighbor's house without permission from our parents and theirs. We could not accept eating at a friend's house without permission.

I am mentioning this because this may sound odd to generations presently. Instruction and boundaries are essential even today.

The difference between the children today is that they are more likely to have both parents working and less unstructured and unsupervised time preoccupied with social media, the internet, more games, and more toys and activities outside the home.

The other situation is the single-parent home limited to being with your children if working. I remember such a time after the divorce from the children's father that I had to work and go to college. I was off every two weeks, so we always did extraordinary things together. We were going for ice cream, the Miller Park Zoo, making pizzas, or a movie on campus.

Something was missing, and that was the teaching of God in my home until I started going back to church. I found out this was missing in many impoverished families in the suburbs where a lot was happening: drugs, gangs, poverty, depression, and violence without God being in the equation. In counting the 80 families served that year, about two to three homes went to church on my caseload of 15.

The church is responsible for raising their children in the way they should. The way to go will be explained alone, along with what discipline really is.

Some people are not training children how they should go because most are doing it on their own without the help of God.

It is not new that the thought of young people being unruly is not new. When rock n roll became popular, some parents were not happy. When we purchased a song called "*Funky Broadway,*" my parents did not allow us to play it, but they would sneak to play it when she was not around. We would say everyone is listening to that song. My mother would say not everybody because you are not. Some parents felt Elvis Presley's pelvic thrusts were too seductive and too worldly. I do not know about anyone else, but we could not wear make-up until high school and clothes that were covered. My parents would stop us as we were leaving and not dressed appropriately. Some may have changed when they went to school, but not us, because the school had rules and would call our parents back then. I do not remember much rebellion back then because rebellion was a bad thing for the church, and most of our friends were Christians. It was when we said the preamble, sang America the Beautiful, and repeated prayers at school.

We had a village that raised us and held everyone accountable as families. Discipline in the village or community is to correct children by others, and no one would question the adults who corrected us. Parents were not so sensitive; they felt the adults had our best interests in mind. If they saw us fighting, showing disrespect, or in the wrong place, they could stop us and tell us to go home and call our parents. I felt the community saved us many a time.

Discipline is teaching rather than punishment, even though a few swats on the behind do not hurt. We had many spankings along with teachings. Most associate with this principle of "spare the rod and spoil the child." Biblically, it says, "Teach a child the way they should go, and when they are old, they will not depart from it." (Proverbs 22:6). It is very clear that parents are to teach children the proper behavior and be an example. We, as Christians, are to teach about the righteousness of God. We teach our children to be obedient to authority and respect of others. Ephesians 6:1 advises children to obey their parents in the Lord, for this is right. Honor your father and mother with the first commandments with a promise that it be we with thee, and thou may live long on the earth. It means you obey not only Christian parents but also people who supervise you, such as teachers and people in authority, such as police officers, judges, and Sunday schoolteachers.

I had to mention the Sunday school teacher because I have had experiences with unruly children, and I have gone to the parents and said their children were talking or writing in the books. A parent actually told me that my child said it was not him but another child. I was looking right at the child and asked him to be quiet, which was expressed to her. Her attitude was that I believed him if he said he did not. That would never have happened in my youth. Parents would be upset if a child was unruly in church and reported by the teacher. The hardest thing for me was when a guest visited our church, and her son's watch was stolen. She confronted the child's parent, who took the watch; the surprising thing was that the child had two identical watches he was wearing. The mother stated she had purchased both watches for her son. The other mother was furious and said she would never visit the church again. I watched how the two interacted, and the young boy asked if he could try on his watch and did not give it back. That young man grew up to be killed by a drug dealer he had robbed.

We have a different standard for Christian homes that sometimes can be compromised by the lack of teaching or business of parents that principles of the Bible are put on the back burner. I assumed it was taught in the home, but when asked questions about bible study and prayer with their families, the answer mostly was no. Moses gave clear instructions in Deuteronomy 6:7: "*These words that I command you today shall be on your heart. You shall teach them diligently to your children.*" We are to pass down God's word to the next generation, including the Ten Commandments. The mother at the church knew that when her son was stealing, the eighth commandment says, "*Thou shall not steal.*"

Parents are held accountable for their children's behavior in some situations. It is in the news, and the courts of parents who neglected their son's mental health purchased him a gun where he killed four classmates. The Michigan mother was found guilty of manslaughter, each carrying a sentence of fifteen years; her husband's is facing a separate trial this year.

Some parents are not teaching their children the same principles we were taught. One parent told me her children did not do chores, wash dishes, or clean the house because she did not trust them to do a good job. I did not understand that because, at six years old, I could not wait to help around the house. My mother would allow us to get on a stool to wash dishes, help us if it was not so perfect, and show me how to do it correctly. Her children were older than six years old and had no responsibilities; mom even cleaned their rooms. I asked this mother if they could get the pots and pan from under my sink because I could not bend that low. I informed the pay was good. She hesitated and asked if they were going to lift anything heavy and how long they would be working. Was that all they would do because she did not want me to work them hard? The mom said that was all they would do; she agreed. They were paid twenty-five dollars for a half-hour job each. Why did I ask a mother who did not want her children to do chores? It was because she had confided that she was short on funds until payday and needed gas money for work. I knew they would give her some money. We both benefited because of my bad knees, and I was grateful.

I disapprove of parents not giving their children responsibilities. My siblings and I would have done this for an elderly person for nothing; it teaches work ethics, compassion, and care for others. How did we conclude that you need to pay for everything? Some children are paid to do chores, which is not good; I can understand some big projects around the house or if your child wants money for something special. Children need to learn that the family unit is to work together and everyone has a role to have a cohesive success. They also learn that it takes teamwork to get something done and that cooperation is needed. Work ethics are cultivated along with respect for the unique talents of others. My brother could iron but did not like cleaning; it was a good thing because my brother would put a crisp crease in my pants, and when it was his turn to do the dishes, it was no problem. If you iron my pants, I will do the dishes, hoping it was not his turn. We devised a plan of washing dishes for one week; being four of us doing that chore, we were off a month before our time came back around again.

In talking to youth, many think they may not have the same opportunities we had as Boomers who established wealth through having job security and the ability to own homes. They are afraid of the world, and we are leaving them full of trouble in every area: economics, environment, health, and survival. Some say they must live to the fullest because nothing is guaranteed.

We used to work at a job until retirement when we were 30-50 years old. My grandfather said he worked 50 years at a chemical plant that would have made him well in his seventies. Most companies had medical insurance, pensions, and unions that protected workers. My sister still gets benefits from General Motors after her husband's death. She still has insurance that covers some of her expenses. Now, youth feel college does not mean a good paying job, ending up with college loans. Jobs do not offer the same benefits; they have none or meager amenities.

Many numb themselves with alcohol, drugs, acting out, and suicide. An article by Andre Vale addresses the suicide rate for teens over the last five years, which is on the rise for 15-19-year-olds in the United States.

Much of the blame is on social media, the COVID-19 pandemic, substance abuse, and bullying. He stated it is more complicated than that, which involves racism and socioeconomic status. LGBTGQIA have seriously thought of suicide, and some have succeeded.

This takes on a personal thing for me; my eight-year-old niece took her life after being bullied at school due to teasing about her hair and color. My heart still hurts thinking of how our youth seemed to have more challenges in this age.

What the Bible says about this time is that in the last days, perilous times shall come. 2 Timothy 3:1 Men shall be lovers of themselves, covetous, boasters, proud, blasphemers, proud, disobedient to parents, unthankful, without natural affection, trucebreaker, false accusers, incontinent (lack of control), fierce, and despisers of those that are good. There is proof that we live in a different, challenging time for youth and adults; it can be frightening.

I viewed interviews in Quora Digest, a platform that shares information by collecting insight from various people. The interviews had interesting responses from teens, Gen X and Gen Z, born between 1990-2004. One felt they were no ruder than or disrespectful as a youth during the Vietnam era. They talked about drugs, wild parties, and rebellion against the war. I remember those times, but most knew no one actively involved; I watched it on the news. Everyone feared the future and if their sons would return from the war.

Others felt that parents were not calling children out for bad behavior or correcting them for disrespect. They stated discipline is needed but not happening because parents are busy trying to make a living. That sounds about right due to the fact that more women work outside the home, not so much when I was growing up and would hear Daddy is going to spank you if we were unruly.

I recalled Gerber's baby food slogan, "Children are our most important resource." We should impart all the teachings that would make them good citizens of heaven and earth. We should also be examples of godliness, love, respect, honesty, and integrity.

We should not be seeing our children gathering in the street, causing chaos, living near Chicago, where, on social media, a destination named for teens to meet, causing disorder, confusion, and destruction. Smash and grab is a thing, too, where a car or a group of people make an entrance into businesses and steal merchandise. These were not the activities I grew up with. We stayed busy without electronic games, social media, or money to go out. We were in after-school and church activities, babysitting, visiting friends, and talking about boys.

I know that young people's attitudes have changed, but many of them value what we value. I just listened to a woman in her early 20s on YouTube speaking about the ballet class she taught to 4 and 5-year-olds. She said when she would ask them to do certain things, they would tell her you are not our mother; we do not have to do it. She stated that when she spoke to a parent, she said her daughter did not have to do what she did not want to do. She also said she has special music for ballet, and they ask to hear "Pound Town," a song using language not meant for five-year-olds. She said the girls were twerking at 4-5. She cited it as a lack of parenting and guidance; I agree. She cried, and this broke my heart. She mentioned that this is the reason many teachers are leaving the profession. My daughter did, and understandably, she is a medical student.

We must do better in church by being that example, but you cannot be holy on Sunday or at home. I hate to say this, but some children will tell your story in Sunday school. We need to go back to the principles of the bible so that our children can take over as leaders and good citizens honoring God. Let us get right and make heaven our home. I am ending with a scripture from Matthew 6:10 "*Your kingdom come. Your will be done On earth as it is in heaven.*"

This is powerful because whatever is in heaven, as children in his kingdom, we have peace, love, riches, healing, faith, and the expectation that Jesus is coming back for us. This is not our permanent home but temporal. We are looking toward our eternal home, so do not miss the mark of your high calling.